D1117935

TYPOLOGIA

Frederic W. Goudy

PORTRAIT BUST BY JO DAVIDSON   PHOTO BY KOLLAR, PARIS

Typologia

STUDIES IN TYPE DESIGN & TYPE MAKING

WITH COMMENTS ON THE INVENTION OF
TYPOGRAPHY · THE FIRST TYPES
LEGIBILITY AND FINE
PRINTING

FREDERIC W. GOUDY, L.H.D., LITT.D.

∴

UNIVERSITY OF CALIFORNIA PRESS

BERKELEY · LOS ANGELES · LONDON

UNIVERSITY OF CALIFORNIA PRESS
BERKELEY, CALIFORNIA

◆

UNIVERSITY OF CALIFORNIA PRESS, LTD.
LONDON, ENGLAND

COPYRIGHT, 1940, BY THE
REGENTS OF THE UNIVERSITY OF CALIFORNIA

FIRST PAPERBACK EDITION, 1977
ISBN: 0-520-03308-6 (CLOTHBOUND)
0-520-03278-8 (PAPERBACK)

PRINTED IN THE UNITED STATES OF AMERICA
BY THE UNIVERSITY OF CALIFORNIA PRESS

This book is dedicated to the memory of my father

JOHN FLEMING GOUDY

booklover and teacher
whose library
first made me a lover of books

Preface

TYPOLOGIA *presents more or less graphically my work in type design and describes my own methods of type production. Of course it does more than that; for who, once having begun a book, can resist its own invitations—to quote, to comment, to ponder and amplify? My intention, then, must be not only to say my own say, but also to bring together from widely separated sources the suggestions or statements of others, and to weave them, with the conclusions reached by my own study and experience, into a new fabric.*

Leigh Hunt once said that he did not like a grand library in which to study. Neither do I. I like "to be in contact with my books, to lean my head against them." I find it so difficult to concentrate my thoughts when faced with a wealth of information contained in a large library that I have practically limited my research to the materials in my own modest collection, picking freely from sources within easy reach, and making the most of things close at hand instead of searching for less accessible matter. I trust, however, that I have presented my findings in a manner which will be interesting as well as useful, and that it may not be said of me, as was said of Bagford, that "he spent his life collecting material for a book . . . which he was quite incompetent to write," or, as was said of another, that "he was happiest in his quotations."

"Truth is the property of no individual; it is the treasure of all men." If I perchance borrow without specific credit, like Bacon, who took all knowledge for his province, or [with a little reserve] Marmontel, who said, "I pounce on what is mine wherever I find it," I intend merely to adapt the language of the unwitting lenders when it expresses my own thoughts clearly—to draw from their full pools of knowledge wherewith to swell my own more scanty rills. I thank them all.

If only some fifteenth-century writer had taken the trouble to speak particularly of the types with which he was familiar, or had some early printer, who in those days was usually the founder of his characters, recorded for us the details of their construction at the time when printing was in its swaddling clothes, what a service he would have rendered us. What endless and bootless conjecture and discussion would have been saved had only a few of Gutenberg's leaden types, which "made the thoughts and imaginations of the soul visible to all," been preserved to us. Or if Jenson's "white letters," the beauty of which is poorly exhibited by his weak impressions, could even now by some happy chance be found, that we might examine and study them, how wonderful, how illuminating it would be! It was more than fifty years after the invention of typography before there was a crude representation of a type founder at work, and almost as long before there was any illustration of a printing press. "It is wonderful," said Lemoine, "but it is true, that the only art which can recall all others, should almost forget itself."

My remarks on type legibility and fine printing, as presented in the body of this book, present the conclusions of a craftsman intensely interested in every phase of typography; but my work as a typographer, or as a printer, is largely incidental to my work as a type designer. It is the designer's voice that speaks with least hesitation on all these pages.

The chapters on type legibility are the result of much study, and while the conclusions I present may not be accepted by all, since there is a wide divergence of opinion on the subject among readers of varying intelligence as well as among those who use types in their own work, yet I hope my remarks may encourage serious experiment by some college or university laboratory better equipped to arrive at scientific conclusions than is possible to a mere designer. My work in this direction has been mainly to achieve the utmost legibility for my own types, and I believe that if or when I have succeeded, it has been because I have applied the principles I advocate herein. It is regrettable that the problem of type legibility has received so little attention as thus far it has, and that so little constructive research has been done in this field by type founders, or by critical laboratory technicians familiar with lettering and types, and that serious concern with the question has been left, in too large measure, to a designer whose time and opportunity for research are inadequate to meet the issue fully, and whose interest and enthusiasm must do perhaps more than they should.

The chapter on fine printing is an endeavor to present the significance of printing—to get at the soul of the matter. In it I have tried to set down general principles only, rather than to give practical instructions on the craft. I have made no attempt at "fine writing," a thing beyond my capability; I have tried to present in logical sequence the principles I follow in type design, and the methods which I have evolved in order to produce the types I have designed; and to describe as graphically as possible and as simply as I can the intricate technical processes of type production. Interspersed among the details of design, drawing, pattern making, matrix cutting, and so on, I have endeavored to express a measure of the philosophy developed through the years, and to present the conclusions I have arrived at, in an attempt to relieve what otherwise, I fear, would prove to many readers merely a dry-as-dust account of technical processes.

As a designer of long experience, I feel that I am in a better position to speak with authority on the various phases of type design and manufacture than the mere historian or critic, who obviously cannot enter into the motives or thoughts of a designer since he has never been faced with the problems of type production. Mine is the advantage of having bumped my head on my own work.

Some of the chapters of "Typologia" were intended as magazine articles, written in moments of leisure, and all have been revised for the purposes of this book. Their writing was a source of pleasure to me and

I sincerely hope that the reader will also find pleasure in their perusal. In spite of the personal pronoun which appears so frequently in these pages, I would emphasize that personal exploitation has not been my aim; I feel that speaking in the first person makes my statements more direct and stronger than they would be if written in the third person.

*The book itself, which I have been asked by the University of California Press to write, plan, and supervise, has been set in a new type designed by me & now first employed for the exclusive use of the University—*UNIVERSITY OF CALIFORNIA OLD STYLE. *Its story is told on the pages under the heading "The Story of a Type"* [see pp. 47-63 below].

FREDERIC W. GOUDY

Marlboro, N. Y.
March 8, 1940

Acknowledgments

I SHOULD LIKE to acknowledge here the helpful suggestions of my erstwhile associate MR. C. LAURON HOOPER, and the critical reading of the manuscript by my friend MR. LESLIE A. MARCHAND of Rutgers University.

I would also thank MR. JO DAVIDSON, the sculptor, for his kind permission to present as frontispiece the picture of his plaster bust of me—which was used for casting a bronze, the last work he was able to complete in Paris before the beginning of the present war in Europe.

I would especially thank MR. HAROLD A. SMALL, Editor of the University of California Press, for his kind assistance and interest, and for his painstaking care in the presentation of the text for this book.

A number of the illustrations of the machines, and so forth, are from photographs made for me by my friend MR. EARL H. EMMONS, and I beg to express my appreciation of his kindness.

F. W. G.

Contents

Illustrations

ILLUSTRATIONS

TYPOLOGIA

TYPOLOGIA

1 : By Way of Explanation

MY STUDY of type design and type founding was begun almoſt forty years ago. At that time, little instructive, constructive, or accurate information was easily available with regard to the various steps involved in the making of a face of type; and this dearth of precise information, it seems, has persisted from Gutenberg's time to the present. That section of Moxon's *Mechanick Exercises* [1683] which relates to the subject of type cutting and founding is somewhat out of date; at beſt, it is not of any great value to the beginner seeking information on present-day methods. Until a few years ago, Fournier's *Manuel Typographique*, a much more intereſting treatise, was obtainable only in French. Other works on type making are too general in their scope, or provide too little material in concrete form, to be of much use.

Within the past few years, articles on the cutting of punches for driving matrices have appeared here and there, in articles which in themselves are admirable enough but which are likely to convey a wrong impression as they imply that punch cutting by hand is still the method generally employed, instead of stating frankly that its use is occasional rather than general, and that except for the cutting more or less infrequently of a private type, punch cutting by hand has practically been abandoned. It is true that composing machines—Monotype, Linotype, Intertype, Ludlow, and others—do employ machine-cut punches for driving matrices, but probably more than nine-tenths of all matrices for casting hand-set types are engraved directly without the intervention of any punch at all.

It must not be inferred, however, that punch cutting by hand—that is, by the hand of the artist himself—is something that should be dropped; it would be as correct to say that the art and craft of the wood engraver should be entirely abandoned. I intend merely to emphasize the fact that engraving by machine has usurped somewhat the functions of hand production in the attempt to secure greater speed and efficiency in the production of types.

When writers on the crafts deprecate the displacement of hand-cut punches by the machine-cut ones, what they say often betrays their ignorance. Much that they write is based, indeed, on theory and not on fact. I agree with them up to a certain point, but I would direct their attention to the atrocities produced in the first half of the nineteenth century, when all types were hand cut; there certainly must be something else besides "hand cutting" to give distinction to a type. Too often they confuse the thing itself and the method of its production. The machine has not killed good craftsmanship; the machine in the hand of the craftsman is merely a more intricate tool than any that was available to the earlier worker, and enables him to carry out his own creative idea more exactly than can be done when the work is passed into the hands of artisans employed to perform the various processes singly: they obviously cannot realize fully just what was in the type creator's mind, and therefore cannot carry out the work absolutely in the spirit in which he worked.

I hold that if the final printed result is satisfactory to the creator of it, and to the viewer of it as well, the method of its production is in a sense immaterial. Of course, a bald statement like this requires qualification, but I shall not attempt it at this time; it will probably develop in the course of the pages following.

On an evening in November, 1888, while William Morris and Emery Walker, his neighbor, were walking home together from a lecture on "Printing" by Mr. Walker, Morris said, "Let's make a new fount of type"—and with that casual remark the Kelmscott Press, it may be said, was born. What Morris remarked on that occasion to Walker, I said many times to Mrs. Goudy in the twenty-odd years past, but unlike Morris, who made drawings only for his "new fount of type," I have not only made designs for my types, but for many of them I have also made the patterns and engraved the matrices, work like that which was done so admirably for Morris from his drawings, by the late Edward P. Prince, dean of England's great punch cutters.

In the Literary Supplement of *The Times* [London], for March 23, 1921, George Moore once pointed out that by offering his books for sale in limited editions in advance of their publication he escaped the uncertainties and exigencies of a dependence upon the general book-buying public. He asserted that only by such means could the handicraft of good printing in this mechanical age be preserved. He complained also that the craft of founding type was being killed by automatic type casters and that it was difficult to get "a new fount of hand-made" type. He displayed here a lamentable ignorance of the craft of type founding and the methods by which a type comes into being. He mistook the mere making of a type by hand for its design. When it is exactly reproduced either by hand or by machine, and cast either by hand in a hand mold or in an automatic caster,* I maintain that no one can say certainly from the print itself which method was used to produce the printing surface.

With this digression, I proceed to the purposes of this book and its scope. It has occurred to me that if I might describe from start to finish the designing of a type and the details of making that type—beginning with the designer's mental attitude and ending with the printed sheet, and illustrating each step as graphically as possible—it might prove interesting to many readers who now accept types almost as a matter of course; and it might also throw light on a matter that Moxon says was "hitherto kept so conceal'd among the Artificers of it, that I cannot learn anyone hath taught it any other," and might supply as well some timely information for booklovers and book collectors, who just now seem more interested in such things than ever before.

* Mr. Moore seemed not to be aware of the fact that an "automatic type caster" will cast type from any form of matrix regardless of the design of the type.

II : Books Before Printing

BOOKS are wells of living water, . . . golden urns in which manna is laid up, or rather, indeed, honeycombs; udders most copiously yielding the milk of life; storerooms ever full." So sings Richard Aungervyle, Bishop of Durham [usually called Richard de Bury, born in 1281 at Bury St. Edmunds], who possessed, for his time, the largest and best library in England. His books were not productions of the printing press, as printing was as yet unborn; they were the work of scribes, mostly monks and ecclesiastics. These scribes comprised *antiquarii, librarii,* and *miniatores,* although sometimes all of the different functions might be exercised by one person. Of them, the *antiquarii* ranked highest, their work including the restoration and revision of faulty texts; next were the *librarii,* who were copyists merely, but skilled in the use of the pen; and last were the illuminators, who contributed only to the decoration of the pages. What De Bury said of books suggests that maybe the "Dark Age" in which he lived was not quite so dark as we have been accustomed to think it.

Since the first types were probably based upon the written forms of letters, if indeed they were not actual imitations of them, our study of the steps leading to the invention of printing may well begin with some reference to the hand-drawn letters of the books which preceded printing. It is regrettable, however, that the very first types should have been founded on the Gothic medieval minuscule of Germany, a hand that stood apart from the writings of other countries and never attained the beauty of other national hands. In Italy the refined taste which had produced a more beautiful standard of writing than elsewhere, and had brought it to a high degree of perfection before the end of the fifteenth century, supplied the fine models adopted by the early Italian printers for their types, a taste which without doubt contributed much toward the quality of work that secured firmly the printing supremacy for Italy. German type printing, although the first known, was almost immediately surpassed in Italy, the home of scholarship, and it was Italy that exerted the first great influence on the new art.

Of course, Gutenberg, the probable inventor of printing from movable types, was more familiar with the handwritten books of his own time and country than with those of other countries, and it is possible that his taste in such matters may not have been sufficiently developed to suggest that search might disclose better models than those immediately at his hand. Although the first movable types were an evolution of the letters of the scribes, printing itself was the immediate outcome of the work of the engraver on wood, a craft entirely separate and distinct from that of the scribes.

That we may more readily understand the influences that actually brought about Gutenberg's practical application of movable types, we should also consider briefly the conditions and tendencies of the century that preceded him. Before the invention of movable types, books were, for the most part, in the hands of the rich, who disliked the thought that possession of them might become common. They were lovers of literature also, and believed that to place these precious things in cheapened form was sacrilege; dangerous too, as science and literature in the hands of the common people might lead to argument and to individual thinking, which in turn might foster intellectual development and self-reliance dangerous to established authority. But this attempt to withhold information proved two-edged and brought about the destruction of "copes, vestments, albes, missals, books, crosses and such idolatrous and superstitious monuments" of the Church, as well as the destruction of the very books which the royal commissioners under Elizabeth wished kept from the common herd.

The fierce conflict we now speak of as the Reformation practically constitutes the history of England for more than two centuries and is exactly reflected in the rude censorship of fire that was applied to literature there and on the Continent for a period of nearly three hundred years. Religious antagonism, military barbarism, and unthinking ignorance brought whole libraries to the flames, and oftener by design than by accident. Yet fire, wars, plunder, and suppression could not destroy the desire for learning, nor could wanton destruction at the hands of the ignorant stay the desire for learning or the acquisition of books. The Revival of Learning, that mighty intellectual movement in Western Europe which marked the close of the fifteenth century, was not confined to France; in Italy and England also the rich and cultured were busy collecting books and employing scribes to make new ones.

Clerics like Alcuin of York had exercised a tremendous influence and stimulated in the great monasteries a degree of activity in all branches of letters, comparable only to the stimulus that the universities had received from the Fratres Minores in the thirteenth century, but had not paralleled until the Revival of Learning. It was the Church alone that had encouraged the making of manuscript books, sluggishly perhaps, but nevertheless sufficiently to make ready for the mental activity which increased rapidly in the fourteenth century, and which was, a little later, to demand even more books than the scribes could furnish. The demand for more speed and accuracy than the scribes could provide made some means of more rapid production necessary, and brought about printing—first, the printing of engraved block books, and later, books printed on the newly invented movable types.

The Revival of Learning was inevitable; in the fourteenth century private libraries had begun to increase in size and number, and the collection of books was no longer monopolized by monks and priests. It was then that the meager collection, some say of only twenty volumes, gathered by King John of France for the Royal Library formed the foundation of the great Bibliothèque Nationale at Paris, increased later by Charles V, the son of John, to nine hundred volumes. The Duke of Urbino's library was distinguished for its completeness. All obtainable works were contained in it, each in perfect state; it is recorded that he employed thirty-four transcribers for the duplication of those books that were unavailable by purchase or otherwise. Wealthy patrons gave still greater encouragement to the writers and illuminators and ordered the classics, until then under the ban of the Church, in such numbers that writing reached a high—in fact its highest—state of perfection. With the spread of learning the necessity for books in greater number was apparent. As a first step to increased production printing came—not printing of pages of text in movable types, but the printing of engraved blocks of illustrations to supplement the work of the scribes.

In the John Rylands Library [formerly in the collection of

Cristofon facien die quacunqz tuens :·:
Illa nempe die morte mala non movieris :·:

Millesimo cccc°
xx° anno :·:·:·

ST. CHRISTOPHER. EARLIEST DATED WOODCUT. 1423

THE LATIN LEGEND AS TRANSLATED IS "ON WHATEVER DAY YOU LOOK UPON THE
FACE OF CHRISTOPHER, ON THAT DAY SHALL YOU SURELY NOT DIE AN EVIL DEATH."

the Earl of Spencer] is a curious print from a wood-block, which represents St. Christopher carrying the infant Jesus. This print, discovered pasted in the cover of a medieval manuscript, is possibly the earliest about which there is no doubt concerning the date of production. It came but a few years before the more important idea was conceived that engraved illustrations might be printed in books before the descriptive text was written in.

The common people, denied the Scriptures, too poor to buy manuscript books, too ignorant perhaps even to read them, turned to the prints that were within their reach and understanding for the emblems that represented the visible symbols of their faith. A favorite subject for the engraver in those days was the Dance of Death. To the ignorant these fearful pictures gave complete evidence of the impartiality of the King of Terrors, who drags from their places noble, protesting priest, rich man, or beggar—irony even within the appreciation of the illiterate.

From prints of pictures to blocks which occasionally bore engraved *lettering* with the illustrations was a natural step. A manuscript writer, usually a mere copyist and skilled of course in the making of letters, was not necessarily competent to copy illustrations accurately. To cover his lack of skill in this regard, blocks of wood were engraved by one making engraving his concern, and these could be printed, the illustrations being thus adequately reproduced in every copy. Although it was expedient to go so far, it was still impracticable to attempt the engraving of many lines of text. The new-found ability to print blocks, including occasional lines of text, did, however, suggest the possibility of some quicker method of duplicating the text as well as the pictures. In spite of the time required to engrave whole pages of text, it was occasionally attempted and numbers of books were issued, mostly of a religious character, in which both the text and the illustrations were engraved. These books were made for priests, mostly illiterate, who found the pictures an aid to the memory and suggestive of texts for their preaching. At the same time they were not too high priced for the people [even though they were unable to read them, the Church would not allow books to be put in their hands]. These block books may be classified as "Books of Images without Text" and "Books of Images with Text," to which may be added the Donatuses, or "Books of Text without Pictures."

THE ABBOT
FROM HOLBEIN'S "DANCE OF DEATH"

These xylographic productions, called block books, of which prints like the St. Christopher referred to above were the forerunners, were intended principally for persons whose education was inadequate for the study of the classics. The *Biblia Pauperum*, or Bible of the Poor, is one of the earliest and is typical of the books immediately preceding type printing. It was cheap and designed for those who could not afford the high prices demanded for manuscript books and who probably could not even have read them. It was not, primarily, a book for reading, but a book to be looked at, as the text was subordinate to the pictures, which, no matter how crude, were

Wie vnd in welicher weis vnd form die fünfzehen zaichen
kimen vor dem jungsten tag, wil ich hienach sagen • Durch
grosser grundloser parmherzigkait, vnd überflüssiger liebin wille
die der allmechtig got zu allen menschen hat • So hat er geordi-
meret vnd gemachet • Das dis nachgeschriben fünfzehen zaichen ge-
schehen sullen vor dem Jungsten tag, nach dem vnd das auch die ler-
er beschreiben • Also das alle element vnd geschepfte • von pitterlich-
er angst vnd forcht wegen • des künftigen jungsten gerichtes Vnd
des gestrengen richters zukunft, allen menschen die zu der zeit im
leben sein zu ainer warnung • Das sy auch pillich vordt haben
sullen • vnd ir sünnd vnd missetat püssen • Auch rew vnd laid dar
über empfahen • Vnd das sy ire güte werck nit sparen • bis für dasselb gestreng gericht • Do all sünd offenbar werden • vnd nach der
gerechtigkait gericht werden • Wann doch lauder zufürchten ist,
Das der merer tail der menschen, mer wol vnd recht tün • von forch
wegen der pen, oder des erschrockenlichen gerichtes, oder der mesch
en • Wann lauter durch gottes willen, oder im zulob vnd zu eren,
Vnd hat sand Jeronimus • die selben fünfzehen zaichen genomen
von kriechischen püchern • vnd die daraus zu latein bracht • Als
man geschribens findet bey dem anfang des püchs • Das man
nennet Legenda sancti fratri Jacobi Ordinis predicatorum,
alio nomine hystoria lambardica • Auch schreibt sanctus Lucas
in dem Euangelio • Erunt signa in sole etc • Dasselb ewangelio
list man an dem andern Sumtag, im dem Advent • von etlichen
den selben zaichen • Doch so sind die pücher nit vberain • Ob die
selben zaichen vor dem Endkrist, oder nach im kimen vnd geschehe
sullen • Darzü so beschreibt auch sand Jeronimus nit, ob die zaich
en nacheinander, on alles mittel der zeit kimen • oder langksam
nacheinander sich vollennden sullen • Das alles sullen vnd müss-
en wir dem allmechtigen got enpfelhen ❧

PAGE FROM GERMAN BLOCK BOOK, "DER ENTKRIST" ["THE
ANTICHRIST"], CIRCA 1450

understood by the most illiterate. This book was printed on paper that was good enough for the purpose and cheaper than vellum; the print was on one side of the leaves, two pages from one block, each two printed pages when folded and ar-

UPPER PART OF FIRST PICTORIAL PAGE, "SPECULUM SALUTIS" [REDUCED]

ranged in sequence facing each other and followed by two blank pages.

The Bible of the Poor was misnamed, as it was not intended for the laity, but rather for the use of the preachers. It presented a series of skeleton sermons ornamented with woodcut illustrations to exercise an illiterate preacher's imagination, and suggesting texts to assist his memory. It consisted of forty leaves of small folio, each presenting a picture with extracts from the Scriptures or other illustrative sentences.

Another remarkable block book is called *Speculum Salutis*, sometimes *Speculum Humanæ Salvationis*, or Mirror of Man's Salvation, in which the engraved explanations are much fuller than in the *Biblia Pauperum*. As a manuscript it was popular for two centuries before the invention of typography, and was written for the instruction of mendicant friars. Two Latin editions of the *Speculum* are extant, both without dates, but the illustrations in both are printed from the same blocks. In the one supposed to be the older, the text of twenty-five of the pages is printed from engraved blocks, but the remaining thirty-eight pages with five pages of preface are printed entirely from movable metal types. In the other edition, all the explanatory text is from types exactly resembling those used in the earlier edition.

There are fifteen celebrated block books. Some of the others are *Ars Moriendi* [Art of Dying], *Canticum Canticorum* [Song of Solomon], *Mirabilia Romæ* [Wonders of Rome], but descriptions of these are not here necessary.*

There is in the Print Room of the British Museum a curious little book, four by six inches in size, in which nearly all the letters of the alphabet are formed by the grotesque figures of men. In it the page for the letter *L* shows a young man leaning on a sword, on the blade of which is clearly written the word "London," leading some writers to believe that the work was probably done in England [the exact date of its execution is not known], although the art of engraving in that country was in a very low state at the beginning of the fifteenth century, the probable time. But the engravings in this curious example are much better designed and executed than in other block books of the same period.

The only block book without pictures is the *Donatus*, or Boys' Latin Grammar, named for its author, Ælius Donatus, a learned

---

* For more complete descriptions and the history of the best-known block books, the reader should see DeVinne's *The Invention of Printing*, Cundall's *Wood Engraving*, Pollard's *Fine Books*, Sotheby's *Principia Typographica*, etc.

Roman of the fourth century who was an instructor of St. Jerome. In the *Cologne Chronicle*, 1499, it is stated that "the art of printing, as has been said, was discovered at Mainz, in

GROTESQUE INITIAL "L" FROM A BLOCK BOOK

the manner as it is now generally used, yet the *first* prefiguration was found in Holland, in the Donatuses which were printed there before that time. And from these Donatuses the beginning of the art was taken."

The literary quality of these block books was slight and

the mechanical execution of the printing contemptible. Readers familiar with the beautiful manuscript books of vellum, written in characters that to this day preserve their color, sharpness, and legibility, rated these printed efforts as "literary rubbish," and the printers of them received little or no encouragement from scholars or wealthy patrons.

The multiplication of single sheets on which the block illustrations and text appeared could, moreover, serve only a temporary purpose, and thereby constitute but the steppingstone, as it were, to the invention of movable types, which are the very essence of typography. The first person, then, to whom the idea came that the text or legends of the engraved blocks might be composed from separate engraved letters capable of rearrangement after each use for other texts or legends, fixed the principles of the new art about to be born. From the successful execution of a few words or lines, it was easy to extend the principle to whole pages, and except for the solving of mechanical details the invention itself was accomplished.

FRAGMENT OF A XYLOGRAPHIC DONATUS

But even yet the world was hardly ready for the invention, as the expense of printing a small number of books was too great and the readers too few, although already too many for the scribes to supply quickly. Printing is cheap only when produced in quantity. For a time, handwritten and illuminated books were even cheaper than those printed from wood blocks. Nevertheless, the idea had been conceived and its fulfillment could not be long delayed; whether by Coster, or Gutenberg, or another, the invention itself was sooner or later inevitable.

"Without the humble Donatuses of Haarlem," says Blades, "we should never have had the wonderful Bible of thirty-six lines; and without the persevering and fruitful efforts of Gutenberg during the ten years from 1440 to 1450, mankind would never have been blessed with that art which his creative genius has raised to a perfection which leaves far behind the first and necessarily imperfect attempts of Koster. In a word: Koster gave us Gutenberg, and Gutenberg has given us Typography."

III : The First Types

"THOUGHT," said the seer, "is the property of him who can entertain it and of him who can adequately place it." The brick stamps of the ancient Babylonians and the brass signet of C. Caecilius Hermias foreshadowed movable types; yet it is none the less honor to Gutenberg, who probably was the first to conceive the principle of casting letters in metal, that some germ of the principle itself was known and in use centuries before him. The intellectual activity of his times made "ars artificialiter scribendi" necessary and brought about the practical application of the ancient principle.

The types of Gutenberg, and to a still greater degree those of the Italians, were the natural and inevitable materialized letters of the manuscript writer, supplying to the art about to come into existence its noblest models, which needed but to be formalized and simplified to meet the technical requirements of type founding. The vagaries of the letter artist and the constantly varying whimsicalities which naturally appeared in his work were seldom repeated there, or exactly duplicated to the point of irritation; hence they were entirely acceptable in manuscript. But variations of this kind could not always be carried into mechanically produced types except at prohibitive expense, if indeed the technical difficulties could be overcome; nor would they always have been desirable—too much mechanical repetition would only have produced an effect of tedious mannerism.

The history of the origin of printing is so full of confusion and intricacy, so obscured by irrelevant and distorted details, so lacking in clear, simple statements by contemporary writers, or the survival of any of the ancient equipment of those pioneers, that the student is likely to be misled and discouraged. Notwithstanding the careful investigations of Blades, Reed, Watson, Lemoine, Mores, Hessels, DeVinne, and others, each with adherents, who arrive at different conclusions on important details, the identity of the actual inventor of printing remains still a matter of uncertainty. But whether printing from movable types originated at Mainz, or whether it didn't, does not especially matter; it was from that place that typography spread throughout the civilized world, and it was demonstrated there that it was possible to produce books from types and illuminations as beautiful as the manuscript books produced by the scribes.

Three men were in the main responsible for the development of the then new art, though we cannot precisely say just what share to allow to each. First may be mentioned Johann Gutenberg, the most famous [to whom the invention itself is usually credited], born at Mainz about the year 1400. Of his early life, education, or profession, next to nothing is known. In fact, about all the information we have of him is in connection with lawsuits or with his efforts to obtain money to prosecute his invention. It is from a suit against him for breach of promise that we get our fair working knowledge of what equipment he had for printing.

At one time Gutenberg resided in the deserted convent of Arbogastus at Strassburg. If it could be exactly ascertained how far he pursued his work in the old convent—if, as seems probable, he went as far as the fashioning of matrices [even if matrices were not used for the casting of his types, until he

air dñs m̄. Bñ oīa st locuti. ꝓpham suscita
bo eis de medio frm̄ suoꝛ similē tui, ⁊ ponā
uba mea in ore eī. loquiturq̃ ad eos oīa q̄ ꝓe
po euī. Qui aū uba eī q̄ loquet in nōie meo
audire noluerit ego ultor existā. ꝓpha aut
q̄ arrogantia depuat uoluerit loq̄ in nōie me
o q̄ ego ñ ꝓcepi illi ut dicet. aut ex nōie alieno
z deoꝛ interficiet. Qd si tacita cogitatōe respō
deris quom̄ possim intelligere uibū qd ñ e locut
hoc hebis signū qd in nōie dñi ꝓpha ille ꝓdi
xerit ⁊ ñ euenerit. hoc dñs ñ locutus e. s ꝑ tumore
animi sui ꝓpha ofinxit. ⁊ idcirco ñ timebis eū.

Cum disꝑdit dñs ds. XIX
Tres gñs. etc̃ z tēlinuit e̅ trā. z possidē
eam. habitauisq̃ in urbibz ⁊ in edibz: tres ciui
tates separabis t in medio tre qm̄ dñs ds tui
dabit t in possessionē tenens. diligent uiam.
Et intres equr partes totā tre tue puinciam
diuides. ut heat e uicino q̄ ꝓpr homicidiū psu
gis e quo possit euade. Hec err lex homicide
fugientis cui uita seruanda e. Qui priseit
pximū suū nesciens ⁊ q̄ heri ⁊ nudiustertius null

had returned to Mainz],—then Strassburg might dispute with Mainz for the right to be called the "birthplace of typography." *

Gutenberg was so constantly in need of funds to carry on his business that he took into partnership a goldsmith, the second of the three referred to, John Fust, who furnished large sums toward the working expenses of the firm. From the records of a suit brought by Fust against his partner Gutenberg we obtain our first definite information concerning the history of his endeavors, as the judgment rendered in this suit compelled Gutenberg to give an account of his receipts and expenditures, an inventory of his equipment, and to hand over to Fust all his apparatus to cover his debt. This, of course, dissolved the partnership. Gutenberg left Mainz. Fust continued the business of printing with the assistance of Peter Schoeffer, last of the three, to whom, it is said, are due improvements in the methods of cutting punches and sinking matrices. Schoeffer probably invented the metal mold in which the firm's types were cast, for he was a skilled mechanic.

That Gutenberg was the actual inventor of printing from movable types may never be known for certain. In considering the claims of other countries to the invention, however, we find the evidence for other printers not as substantial as that for him. We have in his favor the evidence of the actual printed books, and documentary corroborative evidence as well. In France, at Avignon, there are certain documents in

* Since Gutenberg spent about ten years, from 1440 to 1450, in Strassburg, it seems reasonable to assume that he was busy there with the details of the development of his idea for movable types. The first fruits of the new art appeared too soon after 1450 to permit of the idea that his work originated in Mainz, although printing itself first appeared there. It is owing to this assumption that almost all the civilized world is paying tribute to Gutenberg and celebrating the 500th anniversary of his invention in this present year of 1940.

the legal archives on which to base the French contention that Walfogel was the inventor, but no books. In Holland, books were printed which are held by some to date from an earlier year than 1454, but there are no documents to support by direct evidence the claims for Coster at Haarlem [1440]. The claims by Italy for Castaldi of Feltre rest only on tradition, as there remain neither books nor documents on which to base a case for him.

One of the earliest allusions in print to Gutenberg is found in the *Chronica Summorum Pontificum*, a book printed by John Philip de Lignamine at Rome, about 1471 [less than five years after Gutenberg's death], which mentions Gutenberg, Fust, and Mentelin as printing books in the pontificate of Pius II [about 1459]. But the printing of block books did not cease entirely for nearly sixty years after the invention of movable types, the latest one being printed at Venice by Andrea Vavassore in 1510.

It is not, however, with the inventor of printing or the history of his business that this study is concerned, but rather with the actual type forms used by him and the first printers. When printing began, the bookmaking practices of the scribes were as law, and printers were reluctant to break away from the customs of their predecessors. Even after printing was in full sway the ornamentation of the printed page remained a separate art—the province of the rubricator.* In many towns this artisan was a member of the guild or corporation of *miniatores* and painted in the initial letters and the borders on the printed pages, and was entrusted also with the writing in of the titles.

---

* Although the early types were based on the best manuscript hands of their time, it is significant that hand lettering as an art reached its greatest point of perfection after the invention of printing.

It is almost entirely from him that such important information as the dates of books is obtained, and not from any statement of the printer or publisher. The reader is left in complete ignorance by the early printers concerning where, when, and by whom a book was produced.

The earliest block books, as well as those printed from types, were made to imitate manuscripts, and often so closely as to deceive the inexperienced. To carry the illusion as far as possible, spaces were frequently left both in the block books and in those printed from types for the insertion by hand of painted initials and illuminations. In the first monument to printing— the Gutenberg Bible—one is not even told that the volume is a Bible ; and this reticence on the part of the early printers seems to have been the rule rather than the exception. A copy of an Indulgence now preserved at The Hague has the date of November 15, 1454, filled in, thus supplying the first authentic date we have on any printed document. The Mainz Psalter has a statement written in by the *rubricator* giving the date [1457].

In many printing offices, scribes were employed as correctors of the press, since their experience in bookmaking made their services valuable; their familiarity with the handwritten books developed the good taste which later was carried into printing, since the same artistic considerations controlled the books produced by the new art. The practice of ornamenting printed books with painted illuminations continued until the beginning of the sixteenth century, although as early as 1480 several books show the first page of text within a woodcut or engraved border printed with the letterpress.

Type, after all, is merely handwriting divested of the exigencies and accidents of the scribes, conceived as forms to be executed in metal, revised and recaſt from the Carolingian writing of the ninth and tenth centuries and formalized to meet the requirements of new materials and new conditions. The early printers borrowed the more economic forms and achieved results of surprising beauty for first attempts, a faĉt which must be attributed directly to the high quality of the models upon which they based their types. Then, too, they did not forget that legibility was the great desideratum, and expended every effort to bring about this result. This quality of legibility is difficult to explain and is not generally understood, since it requires a degree of taste and a knowledge of faĉts not always possessed by the man in the street—who is the person most likely to criticize most severely. The designers of the first types, being more intent on the uses of their productions than upon any display of their own handicraft, shaped their type forms so that the letters combined insensibly into words—the sole elements which the reader should be conscious of.

Certain characteriſtics developed in letters principally because of the materials on which they were formed—the use by the ancient Assyrians of so stiff and sluggish a substance as clay was the primary reason for the cuneiform or wedge-shaped symbols; the waxed surface of the tablets employed by the Greeks and Romans compelled a broken and disconneĉted style of writing; the frail papyrus made a light touch and slender characters necessary,—but when smooth and hard-surfaced vellum was introduced, firm, clear letters with marked contrasts of fine and thick ſtrokes became the fashion. Lettering had reached this stage when the first printers sought models for their types.

In the days before printing, the scribe was born into a tradition; certain forms were already universal and fundamental and actually in the process of growth and development under the hand of each writer who used them. The first printers employed the materials that came ready-made into their hands. The Roman capitals derived by the scribes from the stone-cut forms and bequeathed by them to the printers were accepted with almoſt no alterations. The printers, however, in their anxiety to compete successfully with the manuscript books, adopted the minuscules which had gradually altered from their original forms to meet the exigencies of the writers, and did not question their entire suitability as shapes for reproduction into metal types. Nor did either printer or founder, until printing had been recognized for its own sake, make any attempt to seek or create minuscule forms better adapted to type reproduction than the written characters. For many years, too, after any necessity for their use was apparent, printers retained the abbreviations and contractions of the scribe [see, e.g., the Donatus fragment, p.16 above], as well as the mannerisms of the manuscript book.

Although the firſt types [patterned after the beautiful manuscript forms of the scribes] were designed to meet technical limitations and comply with mechanical conditions, the punch cutter soon drew away from an esthetic standard in pursuit of a utilitarian ideal—and brought about an entire revolution of ideas. In the early days of the craft, when printing was beautiful, writing was its model; whereas today printing is held superior to writing ["writing" as used here means the formal book hands, not the cursive writing of correspondence]. Alfred Pollard asserts that "we may take it as an axiom, that for the first half century of printing *every* fount of type cut was based on some *particular* manuscript.''

The early printer, who often was also the founder of his characters, possessed no tools of precision and no system for any gradation of sizes of his types; but he did nevertheless produce forms that were quaint and pleasing and always sturdily bold. One critic has referred to the types of two printers who worked near Rome in 1465 as not having been "drawn in true proportions," but as modern readers are not even yet agreed upon a faultless standard for the forms of our types or their proportions, we need not be too severe with these early printers for seeming shortcomings. As a matter of fact, their types were the prototypes of our lower-case letters, and are of interest for that reason if for no other. True, their forms were needlessly bold and rugged, even so far as to lack neatness, but the designer of them purposely avoided hairlines or other possible causes of indistinctness and produced type forms that were easily discernible and of marked personality.

Today, most types, except those frankly based on early forms, are characterized by wearisome commonplace regularities and exhibit few of the deficiencies and irregularities that are inevitable when the craftsman is more intent on the design itself than on mere execution. Types of distinction are created by artists only, and not by engineers or artisans—by craftsmen with a knowledge of the technical limitations and requirements of the craft, and by designers who place feeling above the cut-and-dried effect which comes from slavish adherence to workshop traditions. Here I should like to repeat the dictum that the fundamental forms of letters are absolutely fixed and that only slight changes in their general shapes or

in the proportions of their component parts are ever necessary. A fine type possesses always a simple grandeur that
makes it monumental.

The types of Gutenberg and his associates, as well as those
of his immediate successors, were black-letter in form, and
although the Roman letter was in general use for manuscripts
at that time, yet for nearly a century after the invention of
printing, black-letter was the preferred form, not only in Germany, but also in England, France, and Spain. The year 1465
is generally admitted to be the date of the earliest type issue
in Italy. Two Germans, Sweynheim and Pannartz, printed in
that year at Subiaco, near Rome, in a transitional type nearly
Roman in form but Gothic in color or weight. Roman type
letters of a crude form had appeared in Germany as early as
1464, but no fine Roman type had been produced until that
cut in 1470 by Nicholas Jenson, the Frenchman, and in 1475
even he was forced to cut and print from a Gothic type in order
to economize space and paper and so make cheaper books.

In 1458, legend says, Charles VII of France sent Jenson to
study the new art of printing, of which he had heard marvels,
"the King having learned that Messire Gutenberg, living at
Mayence, in the country of Germany, a dexterous man in carv-
ing and making letters with a punch, had brought to light
the invention of printing by punches and types." On his return to France in 1461, Jenson met with a cool reception, for
Charles VII had died, and his son and successor, Louis XI,
did not have his father's interest in printing. Less than ten
years later we find a disgruntled Jenson established at Venice,
where he joined his art as engraver of letters to that of printer.

In 1469, John of Speyer was printing with a fine Roman type, and it is barely possible that Jenson based his famous fount upon it, but if he did, he incorporated new variations that would naturally occur to a good craftsman, and wrought with greater skill because of his long practice as engraver in the French mint. In his article on "The Art of Printing at Venice during the Italian Renaissance," Castellani says that John of Speyer introduced printing into Venice in 1469, using a "very beautiful round character," and that Jenson "formed a character known as round Roman, not very unlike that used by John of Speyer; but somewhat more regular and elegant." It is not known certainly whether Jenson cut his types after coming to Venice or whether he brought them with him from France. Theo. L. DeVinne believed that he brought his model types with him; but after an examination of the types of John of Speyer and those of Jenson, comparing certain essential features of each, similarities more apparent to a designer of types, possibly, than to a student of bibliography, I am inclined to believe that probably it was not John's types that inspired Jenson's; I think each may have used a similar manuscript hand as a pattern. Horatio Brown in *The Venetian Printing Press* specifies differences in the construction of certain letters made by Jenson and John of Speyer, but the differences are minor variations attributable to the personality of the designers, not to any radical differences in design, and the variations are not sufficient to affect materially the similarity of their printing in general appearance. It requires more than the different placing or shape of the dot of an *i*, or the finishing stroke of a lower-case *h* or *n*, to constitute a real difference in design. Neither debased the form of his Roman letter, however, no matter whence his inspiration.

In Italy the Roman form was in more general use than else-where and was the sort used by Ulrich Han, Philip de Ligna-mine, Rubeus, Aldus, Renner, and others. Alfred Pollard has suggested that types in Italy took on a new aspect after 1480 and do not seem to be founded on manuscript forms. He sug-gests, and reasonably, that type cutters had by then become well enough practiced in their craft to discard their manu-script models and give their own ideas freer play. It is a fact, however, that while their later types are mechanically more perfect, many of them lack, for us, much of the charm of the earlier letters.

The early Roman types used first in Latin text gave a smooth and pleasing appearance in composition by the lack of such letters as *k* and *w* and other more or less ugly consonants which break up our English words unpleasantly. An exact imitation of even the best of the Venetian models, when used to print English text, might display accidental peculiarities unnoticed in their original use that would savor of affecta-tion and would require some modifications to make them en-tirely satisfactory for modern uses.

iv : The Force of Tradition

THE TYPES of Garamond, Bodoni, Didot, Caslon, Baskerville, and other well-known faces [or type founders' imitations of them] have been available for years to printers generally,
and practically any piece of printing required can be done adequately and satisfactorily with one or another of them, old as
they are. It is no less true, however, that the wearing apparel of
the citizen of Shakespeare's time was adequate and suited to
his times, and might, so far as practicality is concerned, be just
as suitable for our own. But there is the matter of "style" to
consider, and just as in the matter of clothes, styles in types
change capriciously.

Printers have been loyal to the masterpieces of the early
craftsmen and have hesitated to heed seriously the experiments
of modern designers of types. But why carry loyalty to the point
of disregarding all newer designs, when possibly some may
be equally meritorious? Is it true, as has been said, that designers are at best mere amateurs and their art comparatively
a humble one? I do not hold to this view.

The type designer is no mere amateur. The amateur is concerned mainly with problems of esthetics; the professional is
concerned with the problem of a livelihood; the type designer
must attempt to solve both. It is true that type design as a
separate vocation is practiced by few independent craftsmen,
because hitherto, for such work, too little remuneration has
been offered to attract artists capable of original effort.

While there is just now a greater interest in the design of
types than ever before, there seems also to be a concerted move-

ment by many printers to use letter forms which plainly show that the designers of them have chosen to disregard or override [unwisely] the best traditions of the type designer's art. For myself, I firmly believe that the best types for our use must be newer letter forms based on the shapes fixed by tradition, fresh expressions into which new life and vigor have been infused, creating new types which are characterized by severe restraint & which exhibit the poise and reposeful quality that are always pleasing. But, I am asked, just what do we mean by "tradition"—what is "tradition" that we should bow to it?

The need or demand for a new or useful thing exacts careful consideration for its construction and its material as determined by what it is to do, and at the same time excites a desire for its ornamentation, both construction and ornament reaching comparative perfection only after slow and gradual evolution.

The choice of details exercised by a worker with fine and delicate perceptions will endow with a special beauty any work of utility he touches; a vulgar workman can never decorate, because his perceptions are vicious and his choice and selection of details are erroneous. The artist expresses himself in the choice he makes.

An ornamental form once found delightful invites repetition; it is handed on from generation to generation, until finally, firmly established by use, it has become a traditional form. Tradition itself, however, is merely the ladder by which we climb, the working hypothesis that saves us from despair because it is all we have to go on. If we obey tradition, even though our efforts at first are crude and archaic, our work will rest upon a firm foundation.

Almost always, early ornamental forms were symbolic; though their original significance may later have been overlooked or forgotten, frequently with loss of much of their interest or character, there still remain of them today the abstract developments in which inhere the dignity or simple beauty that will enhance the appearance of the thing adorned.

There was a time when the artist was both artist and craftsman, himself the executor of the things his genius created. His imagination and handicraft were much occupied with devising and making more beautiful the necessary implements of everyday life. His imagination developed with increased and varied experience; the technical difficulties he met, and his mastery of them, led to the selection of the tools and methods which he found best adapted to the work in hand, and inevitably brought about the formation of noble traditions. I do not mean by this that tradition is a mere collection of cut-and-dried rules or precepts by which we are to work; tradition is a rich and varied store of tried methods and improved processes.

While rules and precepts show beginners what others have found it wise to do, tradition itself goes more deeply into the very principles of art and life. The aim of art is to make a useful thing beautiful as well as useful; tradition not only teaches the best way that has been found to do it, but shows also the metes and bounds of man's endeavor reached at the moment, the walled boundaries within which the imagination of the craftsman may have full sway. His work need not be dull or uninspired because seemingly restrained. A wholesome respect for the thought and effort that has brought about a tradition will go far to prevent the perpetration of eccentric solecisms.

Tradition invites spontaneous excursions of individual taſte and fancy within her established limits, yet leaves the artist free to attempt consistent, reasoned, and dignified essays to enlarge her borders. Since no one man can possibly exploit all the treasures brought to light, others who follow him will find ample room to exercise all the originality of which they are ca-pable. It is in the fire of research and study, link by link, that the chain of tradition is forged.

Juſt as a language, said Bishop Trench, "will often be wiser, not merely than the vulgar, but even than the wisest of those who speak it," so a tradition which has embalmed and pre-served the thoughts and experiments of generations of workers must be superior to the efforts of beginners in a craft, or of those ignorant or disdainful of the requisite knowledge.

The beginnings of any handicraft take note only of pleasing utility, but as requirements become more and more complex and must be satisfied, and new ideas come which muſt find expression, greater subtleties of design and invention appear, until finally the tradition of the craft has reached us adorned & enriched for our use. Yet tradition is not to be followed solely for its own sake; the logical framework of a craft, the general rules that control it—these with all the acquisitions of thought, feeling, & experience are ours to carry forward by new essays, and the additions we make will enlarge the legacy of tradition which we may bequeath to those who follow us, just as we inherit and use the traditions that have come down to us; we benefit by the labor of the skilled artisans who have blazed the way; in our hands is the key with which to unlock those ancient ſtorehouses with their accumulated treasures, the gold of truth dug from the mines of the past. To accept medieval tradition, however, without adding something of ourselves to it, is mere affectation; "it is no longer tradition if it be servilely copied, without change, the token of life." The dogmas of tradition, therefore, are flexible and are to be enforced lightly, that they do not wholly imprison us.

Genius is the expression of a strong individuality, and extends the limits of a tradition instead of attempting to invent a new one. Genius cultivates old fields in new ways. While a designer of strong artistic personality may modify the laws of tradition more or less according to his strength and ability, he is nevertheless seldom free from its influence; in fact, few great artists have ever become great by deliberately disregarding tradition. Once in a blue moon an individual designer will distinguish himself by his personal choice and unusual treatment of details, by some new thought or method, or by a fresh sentiment or point of view; his fertile imagination finds new expressions for new feelings and thereby his work marks a new epoch in art.

Happily, the imaginative faculty is not confined to the few, since in some degree it belongs to all, a common heritage that grows with use. A sound tradition directs the imagination and confines it safely within the bounds of reason. On the other hand, original and creative invention of a high order is a form of imagination that belongs to comparatively few workers.

Memories of beautiful things that at some time have deeply stirred our admiration are the seeds from which invention springs; in the mind are stored up impressions to be created into new forms, the splendor or poverty of which is determined by one's mental strength and ability. Invention demands that we soar above mere caprices of fashion.

Years ago, in an article on "Style in the Composition of Type," Mr. Updike said that "style in printing does not permanently reside in any one manner of work, but on those principles on which almost all manners of work may be based." This, to my mind, is only another way of saying that tradition is a safe basis upon which to work; for a good tradition is the ultimate result of the application of fundamental principles. The recognition and successful application of those principles has been the mark of all the great printers and type designers of the past, as it must be of all those of the future. Types may present an appearance of novelty without necessarily losing the grace of tradition.

The immediate business of an artist may be the practice of but one craft, but unless his interest is concerned with the whole range of art, he will fall short of attaining the fullest ideals of his own. If he would express in his work vivacity, charm, invention, grace, and an interesting variety, he must cultivate a fine taste and a liberal spirit by a study of the masterpieces of all the arts. He will thus gain a breadth and depth of vision, an insight into fundamental principles, and the courage to face technical difficulties. He must learn, however, not to imitate masterpieces, but rather to follow the traditions on which masterpieces are reared. Tradition, we see then, is a matter of environment and of intellectual atmosphere. The continuous efforts of generations of cunning workers along one line led naturally to the accumulation of knowledge, increased ability to design, and greater manual dexterity, so that certain ways of doing things have come to be recognized as the best. Therefore, it is only by following good and tried traditions that craftsmanship of the highest order can come.

v : What Type Is

PRINTING—'that most noble of the Mechanick Arts, being that to which Letters and Science have given the Precision and Durability of the printed Page'—was invented in response to a growing demand for speed." Someone has said that "the moment that marked the liberation of words from the limitations of the medieval scribes also marked the beginning of modern civilization," the moment being, of course, the invention of movable types. In the type founder's craft the moment that marked the elimination of the founder's punch and introduced the machine-cut matrix, marked too, in a way, the severance of the connection which until then had existed between artist and artisan, that intimate relation which should exist in all art that creates useful things and makes them pleasing by appropriate decoration.

The immediate predecessors of type—the manuscript letters of medieval times—were shaped for easy reading. The first types followed them in form, but because of technical and mechanical limitations they had first to be simplified to meet the exigencies of use—not, however, at the expense of legibility or beauty. Although the first types were based on the scribe's writing, probably with the intention of deceiving readers into the belief that they were manuscript, or, at any rate, of supplying type forms similar to the written letter forms with which readers were already familiar, the type forms themselves gradually drew away from their models as printers discovered that one shape was as easy to cut and found [and print] as another. Later, to conserve space, types were often unduly compressed

and reduced, thereby losing much of the beauty that at first
was the great desideratum.

Manuscripts were, in many respects, rivals of the early printing as well as its type models; in fact, printing was simply
another method of writing, differing in means only. Printers
often insisted that their work was indistinguishable from
manuscript or superior to it. In Paris, it is said, the first printed
books to reach that city were actually passed off as manuscripts.
The scribe's letter that supplied the model of the desired type
to be cut in metal did not always exhibit the expected and
wished-for beauty in the type itself, because the metal workers
who undertook to draw the letter, cut punches, and fit matrices
were not always equal to the task. As type cutting was a new
craft, there were no precedents for them to follow, no traditions
to direct their efforts; they created their own precedents. It was
only when types were produced by craftsmen who were artists
also, workers who appreciated the subtleties of letter forms,
and who gave intelligent supervision to every stage of type
founding and letter cutting, that types began to display a beauty
and character of their own.

The perfect model for a type letter is altogether imaginary;
there is no copy for the designer today except the form created
by some earlier artist, and the excellence of a designer's work
depends entirely upon the degree of imagination and feeling
he can include in his rendition of that traditional form. Just
as the scribe's writing was adapted from the early lapidary
letters, simplified by dropping everything difficult to shape
easily with the pen and yet retaining the essential letter forms,
so types are the materialized letters of the scribes, that is, handwriting divested of the scribe's vagaries and whimsicalities,

conceived as forms to be cut in metal, and needing only to be simplified and formalized to meet the new and enlarged conditions of use. It is regrettable, perhaps, that our first types should have followed those written letters so closely in form. Suppose, instead, they had followed the earlier Greek designs. In that event our lower-case letters would probably be of more gracious line, their parts in more perfect proportion and contrast, and quite possibly they would show less of the crude and barbarous angularity which they now exhibit. On the other hand, they do show a robust strength and virility and character that make them more legible and more interesting than they might have been, had they been derived from a purer and more beautiful archetype.

Although letters are the individual signs that compose the alphabet, each one signifying primarily but one thing—what letter it is—and beyond that having, until joined with other letters to form words and sentences, no significance, they do have, in addition to the main purpose of making thought visible, a decorative quality which is theirs as a whole, quite aside from any ornamental treatment of the separate characters or their arrangement—a quality that constitutes the graphic art itself. This decorative quality intimately concerns the type designer and is the outcome of feeling rather than the result of any conscious effort on his part to attain it.

But form alone is not enough; type must show life and power, that is, expression. Many types have correct enough forms, yet lack entirely that vibrant quality of life and vigor which comes naturally from the hand of a craftsman who is intent on personal expression and is not merely attempting to display his draftsmanship or striving for an exact and precise finish.

Types, too, must have character. But in what does type character consist? A writer in a recent magazine article has said that "imperfections are the foundation of a type design's character." As I have said elsewhere, I believe that if a design has character, it is in spite of its imperfections, not because of them. There is a wide gap between freedom of drawing with natural irregularities of execution, and imperfections *per se*. No, character is not gained by imperfections of handling or eccentricities of form or bizarre details. Then how is it attained? Is it something got by conscious effort, or is it rather a by-product of the designer's own individuality or personality, something he doesn't deliberately and consciously strive for, or is it, again, some innate thing which is in his work because of his unique personality?

For myself, I believe that type character is the outcome of a sincere attempt by the designer to fashion his letters upon a sound tradition and then to add such subtleties in the handling of his lines and curves as are within his ability and power, qualities which are unconsciously produced in his drawing and controlled by his innate good taste and feeling and imagination. Character in types has to do with the impression made by the individual forms, their proportions, and the intangible something in them that makes the letters of each word hang together to form an agreeable whole; each letter with a quality of completeness, and not made up of bits taken here and there; each a shape with an air of its own, with graces not too obvious, and with no affectation of antiquity. When technical conditions are fully understood, frankly acknowledged, and fairly complied with, a long stride toward character will have been made.

When a type design is good it is not because each individual letter of the alphabet is perfect in form, but because there is a feeling of harmony and unbroken rhythm that runs through the whole design, each letter kin to every other and to all.

One writer, in speaking of modern type design, says, "It is doubtful whether the type designer benefits from a close study of hand lettering," meaning a study of the manuscript hands of the past. In the main I am inclined to agree with him. I do find manuscript letters intensely interesting, but only occasionally do they suggest new type expressions to me. As a general thing I prefer to get my suggestions from a study of the earlier types that appeal to me, realizing of course that the types which I most admire were quite probably inspired by the very manuscript hands which I do not find of much use in my own work. With complete independence of calligraphy I attempt to secure, rather, the negative quality of unpretentiousness, and strive for the pure contour and monumental character of the classic Roman letters in the spirit of the best traditions, and avoid, as far as I am able, any fantastic quality or any exhibition of self-conscious preciosity.

My friend, Stanley Morison, has said, "The good type-designer knows that, for a new fount to be successful, it has to be so good that only very few recognize its novelty. If readers do not notice the consummate reticence and rare discipline of a new type it is probably a good letter. But if my friends think that the tail of my lower-case r or the lip of my lower-case e is rather jolly, you may know that the fount would have been better had neither been made." I am not sure that I accept his dictum completely, but inversely I have often said that when one friend or critic has found fault with the tail of an *r* or the lip of an *e* of one of my own types, I have scarcely considered the criticism, but if a number of critics should fix on the same points, I would be inclined to reconsider my drawing. If the tail of one of my *r*'s should prove "rather jolly" I would not kill it because of that fact, provided it took its harmonious place in the fount and did not invite undue attention because of its jollity.

It is hardly possible to create a good type face that will differ radically from the established forms of the past; nevertheless it is still possible to secure new expressions of life and vigor. The types in daily use, almost without exception, betray too fully the evidences of their origin, and do not always follow the best traditions. It requires the skilled hand, the appreciation and taste of the artist, and the trained mind of the student to select suitable models which may be adapted to our use and to which we may give new graces suited to our times. I have made designs that reverted for their inspiration to the lapidary characters of the early Romans; others that were based on the classic types of Jenson, Ratdolt, Aldus; still others that were suggested by the scribes' hands which were also the source of the types of those masters; and now, in the autumn of my labors, I draw with practically no reference to any of the sources mentioned; relying largely on the broad impressions of early forms stored up by years of study and practice, and governed by a technical knowledge of the requirements of type founding and typography, I attempt to create those impressions into new designs of beauty and utility.

We should study the early types in order to know them, to increase the material for our future use, or even copy them if we do not allow our copies to become the end desired instead

of the means to an end. We should study them not merely to
revive or imitate them because we admire them indiscrimi-
nately, but rather so that we may piece together the broken
threads of tradition, there intact, and finally to adapt them
to our increased mechanical facilities and thus create for them
a wider currency. "Only an inventor knows how to borrow."

VI : The Story of a Type

I AM ASKED so frequently how I begin a new type, where I get my inspiration [if "inspiration" is not too important a word in this connection], and very often why I use this form or that rather than another, that I believe the story of the type used herein will illustrate concretely the matters, covered generally in the rest of this book, which relate to the type designer's problems. It is the story of an actual commission to design a type, and it suggests, too, the thousand and one mental quirks and turns, "the various moods of mind that through the soul come thronging," so difficult to recall, but very real in the process of bringing a new type to life, and varying with every new essay. The story serves also to fix definitely the matter of its provenance [a matter of some interest to me, since I find that already in my own lifetime some of my early designs are credited to others], and this account is therefore of bibliograhic interest.

In my library in a bookcase where I keep the books which interest me as possessing special typographical details, or as products of private presses, or as typographic curiosa, rather than for any literary quality they may have in them, I found recently [while I was looking for another book] a copy of John Milton's *Comus and Other Poems*, published in 1906 by the Cambridge University Press and printed in a hodgepodge of incongruous types. And the thought occurred to me that no university with a university press, so far as I could recall, possessed a type which had been designed for its exclusive use, and I could not help wondering why the head of some great university had not

tried to gain greater distinction for its publications by acquiring a type which should be the university's own.

A little research showed me that the earliest university
presses were in private hands, and not until the Reformation
did it come about that the Earl of Leicester, Queen Elizabeth's
favorite, thought to start a learned press at Oxford similar to
the one already set up at Cambridge. Leicester was Chancellor
of Oxford from 1564 to 1588; in a book published in 1585 he
is specially mentioned as the "founder of the new press," and
it probably was the first press at Oxford, since there seems to
have been no recollection at that time of any earlier printing
done there.

In the history of the Oxford Press from 1568 to 1586, little
mention is made of the types used in its publications, except
now and then to say "type No. 2" or "type No. 3," as the case
might be, or, in the books printed between 1568 and 1580,
"type No. 1 only." But I do not find anywhere any specific
statement that the types were its exclusive property with respect to their design. The late Horace Hart [Printer to the University in 1900] said that "the earliest Oxford printing was
executed with characters brought from Cologne." For later
printing, prior to the coming of Bishop Fell, types from Germany, France, and Holland were used; no type founding was
practiced in England before 1637.

Dr. John Fell, Bishop of Oxford from 1675 to 1686, was an
ardent promoter of learning and it was he who first established
a type foundry at Oxford in the year following his presentation
of valuable matrices to the Press. But these matrices, pur-
chased by him in Holland, were not specially designed for the
University, although they were for its exclusive use. Many of

the matrices and punches owned by the Press were discarded as fashions in typography changed; they were not destroyed, but many disappeared, being neglected. Those for casting the Fell types remained *perdu* for about a hundred and fifty years, when they were revived; even now they are in occasional use.

The Fell types have long had a peculiar interest for me and it was upon them that my own "Kennerley" design in 1911 was based; note, I say "based" but I really mean "inspired," as comparison of my type with the Fell letter will disclose little more than an identity of spirit, rather than any particular similarities in design. Of the Fell types it has been said that "they represent a form of letter which is considered beautiful because of its irregularity. The Fell types preceded Caslon, and are probably the parents of the [Caslon] old face and the 'old styles' of today." I do not agree with any writer who says the beauty of the face lies in its irregularities; the irregularities are the result of accidents of type founding, or of the ineptness of the punch cutter, and do not constitute a part of the design. Imperfections in type founding are not the foundation of character in a design; if the type has character it will show in the type in spite of any imperfections, not because of them. There is a great difference between freedom of drawing and infelicities of handling or mere imperfections of manufacture. No, character is not developed through any eccentricities of handling, nor is it to be acquired by conscious effort. The Fell types, to me, represent a sincere attempt to follow a sound tradition by a punch cutter whose work was the product of his innate good taste and feeling.

It was my great pleasure in 1925, on the occasion of a visit to Oxford, to have Dr. Johnson, Printer to the University, bring out from the vaults some of the matrices of this type that I might actually hold them in my hands and mentally compare them with matrices of my own making. Sometime in 1910, my friend Mitchell Kennerley, the publisher, brought back from London a copy of *Notes on a Century of Typography at the University Press, Oxford,* 1693-1794, by Horace Hart, printed in 1900 in an edition of 150 copies; it is the specimen of 1693 showing the Fell letter which served as my inspiration for the type I designed and first used for H. G. Wells's *Door in the Wall.*

But let us get to the start of our present story.

Samuel T. Farquhar, Manager of the University of California Press, wrote me under date of December 18, 1936, saying, "One of the Regents of the University who is much interested in printing and the development of the Press suggested to President Sproul that we should have our own type face," and adding, "Would you be interested in considering designing a face for us?" The receipt of this request was a matter of moment for me—here was the thing I had long wanted to do, to attempt a face for the publications of a great university.

In my reply, of December 30, 1936, I wrote: "It is a coincidence that your inquiry should follow so closely upon the heels of the practical completion of my one hundred first type design, a face that I hope may prove the best of its kind in my long list of faces, and strangely enough it is exactly the type I should have worked toward if I actually had had the University in mind while employed on it. So far I have shown it to *no one.* It would be futile to send the drawings to you, as my experience shows me that no one, not even myself, can entirely visualize the effect or appearance of a book type from drawings, and photographic reductions are so inadequate and deceiving that I do not trust them. I will do this, however, assuming that the matter is being considered seriously by you—I will engrave a sufficient number of 14-point characters from my drawings and cast enough type from the matrices to enable you to set up words and lines which will indicate pretty accurately the general effect of the face as a whole. This, of course, will involve making patterns, both master and working, engraving matrices, and casting type, an amount of work that I, ordinarily, would hesitate to undertake on the mere chance of a commission, without compensation. The suggested opportunity to become, in a way, identified with an outstanding university [I, unfortunately, having no collegiate or university training] leads me to offer to go farther in the matter than otherwise I would be willing to go.

"I imagine that for your work, in addition to the usual roman capitals, lower-case, points, and figures you would want also the small capitals, and possibly an italic to accompany the roman. I am assuming, too, that you would want a book face, not one for display use, and that it would need to be simple in form, dignified, distinguished, and, above all else, easily legible—a type which the University would take pride in using for its finest and most important productions."

In April or May I decided that a little vacation would be good for me and I went to Los Angeles. A day or two after my arrival, the Los Angeles Times got news of my presence there and put a little notice on its front page. The next day, I received a telephone call at my hotel—the old Gates Hotel, where I had stopped on my first visit to Los Angeles in 1915—from Edward A. Dickson, one of the Regents of the University of California, asking if he might talk with me, telling me that he had been

a newspaperman and was interested in type, and of his connection with the University. We had a pleasant visit and two
days later he drove me out to the Clark Library. On May 12th
he wrote to Mr. Farquhar: "By a peculiar coincidence, I called
on Mr. Frederic W. Goudy a few days ago to talk over my favorite subject of type. To my surprise and pleasure I found that
he is in California on your invitation to consider the matter
of cutting a type for the University of California. This is a subject that long ago I discussed with President Sproul, but it
never occurred to me that you might be able to secure the dean
of the world's type designers for that purpose. Gutenberg designed the first movable type in 1440. What an opportunity—
celebrate the 500th anniversary of that event by having Goudy
cut a type for the University of California, to be first used in
1940 in the printing of an appropriate memorial."

To cut the rest of the long story short, the final word came
in a letter from Mr. Farquhar, dated December 10th: "President
Sproul telephoned me yesterday and asked if I still wanted the
type and I told him that I did most decidedly. Thereupon he
told me to go ahead and get it."

I at once started making patterns for the type referred to in
my letter to Mr. Farquhar in December, 1936, cutting a number of matrices to cast enough type to set a few paragraphs
to show him. On December 22d he wrote that he would be in
Marlboro on Saturday the 15th of January, 1938. By January
8th I was able to get a proof of the type I planned for the University and—my heart sank—it was one of those disappoint-
ments that occasionally [thank God, only "occasionally"]
come through the inability of any designer to visualize completely the effect of large drawings as type. What to do next?

Time was short. But luckily I do not long remain downcast. Like the doctors, I can bury my own mistakes, and that's exactly what I did, figuratively at least. I studied the proofs to see if any salvage was possible, but decided reluctantly to hide away the drawings and proofs and begin anew. On January 13th I had completed drawings for a new design, new master and work patterns, new matrices, and new proofs. This time I was almost satisfied that there was nothing so bad a little doctoring would not put it to rights. Mr. Farquhar arrived, and he seemed pleased with the results. He told me afterward that if I had shown him the discarded design *first* he would have accepted it—but not after he had seen the new one.

By March 31st I had finished the larger part of the italic. Mr. Farquhar wrote on May 17th that he had "examined the smaller sizes carefully and liked the italic as well as the roman. . . . Go ahead with the job." On August 25th he wrote: "What is the status of the type? Publicity is appearing constantly in the printing journals and I am being questioned about the date of completion. *Personally we are in no hurry whatsoever, so do not put yourself out.*" In my reply, written September 13th, I said: "I still have about one-fourth of the italic to draw or make patterns for, but now that the weather better permits work, things will soon begin to clean up. I am glad you are not forcing my hand or nagging me—your consideration will show favorably in the final result. . . . I have the 18-point mats cut as far as patterns go—have figures and tied letters and a few special characters to perfect yet. . . . This design of yours is very much on my mind—I'm trying hard to make it a magnum opus, and maybe the very effort is preventing more rapid progress—maybe magnum opuses aren't made so, consciously."

When I began the new design, I put out of my mind the dis-
appointment of the first proofs and started afresh. Should I
attempt to design a face for general use, or something more
limited in scope—something more exotic, as it were?

I decided to make general use the main thing, and I would
attempt to give to the face the utmost in distinction compat-
ible with such use, keeping especially in mind the wish to
secure the greatest legibility in the type and a degree of beauty
as well. I did not attempt any radical departures from good
tradition. I believe, however, that some of the individual characters present a measure of novelty, yet in complete harmony
with their more conservative kinsmen in the font. In short, it
was my purpose to attempt a type face which would present
a new type expression *in mass*, not by drawing forms of letters
radically different from the accepted shapes, but rather by including in them those fine and almost imperceptible qualities
of design which mean so much in the massed effect of the type
page. Whether or not I have succeeded, this book must give
the best answer.

On November 7th I could report progress: "I expect this
week to finish practically all the roman patterns for cutting
punches in 8-, 10-, and 12-pt. It has meant more work than
I'd anticipated to develop a *raised* pattern that would be fool
proof, expeditious, and accurate, but I finally got it and have
a number ready for cutting and the balance traced and in process of making. I've been able to introduce some minor refine-
ments into the design at the same time [without changing
the general effect] which I think you'll appreciate. I'm getting
anxious to finish up now, so I can get out in early spring and
see you making use of it."

For an italic type to accompany the roman, I attempted to draw a refined letter, yet not, I hope, one which may be called prudish. If any departures are evident, a study of them will disclose the fact that the departures do not violate good tradition. Some letters are a bit exuberant, but they are, I think, entirely in harmony with the roman letters. As an italic is seldom used for masses of text, but rather to emphasize a word or phrase in the roman matter, or sometimes merely to give a lighter touch, I have allowed myself to incorporate here and there in my fount some forms more or less fanciful.

I have attempted also to preserve a certain regularity in the irregular forms while maintaining a severity in line and have made a letter which is individual and at times even presents willful traits that should enhance interest in the design.

A criticism that is made of many types [and properly, too] is that their parentage is ill bred. I do not believe that criticism can fairly be made of the italics in the present fount.

The next step was the preparation of the master and working patterns for cutting punches for the composition sizes, 8-, 10-, and 12-point, which were to be cast on the Lanston monotype machine. I had already engraved trial matrices in 12-point for the roman and italic and had planned to engrave matrices for the larger display sizes, 18-, 24-, and 30-point, myself, and furnish the actual type for these sizes for the use of the Press, but unfortunately for me, in the early morning of January 26, 1939, my workshop burned to the ground, and all my equipment, drawings, patterns, and stock of matrices were utterly ruined. Fortunately, I had completed all the master patterns, and had engraved the working patterns some weeks before and forwarded them to the Monotype Company for use in cutting punches. The drawings, with the exception of one sheet of italic showing the letters *d, o, n, r, i, l, f, fl*, together with two master patterns for the lower-case roman letters *p* and *j* which I had sent to Philadelphia with the work patterns, were completely lost. As I had no patterns, it became necessary to have the Monotype Company cut punches also for the sizes I

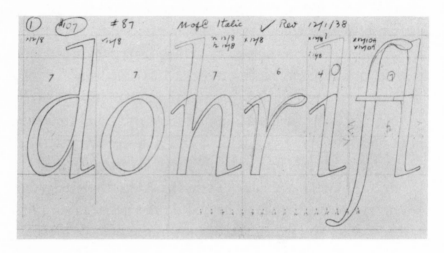

THE ONLY DRAWING SAVED FROM THE FIRE OF JANUARY 26, 1939

had planned to do, and I was unable to make slight changes in the proportions of some characters which the arbitrary set-widths and fitting required in matrices for the die case—changes that would, I felt, measurably improve those characters.

    Some weeks after the fire, it occurred to me to ask the Mono-type Company to pull some flat proofs of the metal work patterns, and this was done. Since the pattern for a monotype punch-cutting machine requires a raised letter form in metal, the face showing the character itself direct just as a print from a type would appear, the proofs which I asked for would show the face of the pattern letters turned over, that is, backward.

For the purposes of illustration, the reproductions of the pattern proofs have themselves been "turned over" also, to display the design as drawn and illustrate them more exactly than a print showing them backward, which the proofs from the patterns would do. These proofs constitute as nearly as possible the design itself in characters reduced from the 7½-inch drawings. They show the letters exactly as drawn, except for my inability to reproduce an absolutely *square* corner with a revolving cutter, but as the diameter of the finishing cutter was approximately 0.025 to 0.030 inch, and its cut was, in turn, reduced, for 12-point, in the matrix, to one-fifteenth the work-pattern size, a corner was produced so nearly "square" as to require examination under a microscope to show the slight roundness that was invisible even to keen eyesight.

When the new type began to assume its final form, the question of a name for it came up. During the process of cutting punches, a number was sufficient identification as far as the requirements of manufacture were concerned; but while a number is probably all that is necessary to designate mere things in sequence, for a creation designed to please your fancy, or to appeal to your esthetic sense, it is far too prosaic. Mr. Farquhar suggested "Californian" in place of my own suggestion of "Berkeley," which to me has an aristocratic connotation; but "Berkeley" was discarded, mainly because it might seem to limit the possession and use of the type to one of the University of California's seven campuses.

During the weeks required for the type's production it was known as "Californian," both in my correspondence with the Press and in the publicity which the new type was receiving in the trade journals; but I never quite liked the name. It seemed

ABCDJ
EFGHI
KLMQ
NOS&

DESIGNS FOR UNIVERSITY OF CALIFORNIA OLD STYLE
REDUCED FROM THE 2$\frac{1}{2}$-INCH WORK PATTERNS

PYWU

packm

dyogih

ffle?245

DESIGNS FOR UNIVERSITY OF CALIFORNIA OLD STYLE
REDUCED FROM THE 2½-INCH WORK PATTERNS

BABES
MORK
RYIT &
QUJNT

DESIGNS FOR UNIVERSITY OF CALIFORNIA OLD STYLE ITALIC
REDUCED FROM THE 2$^1/_2$-INCH WORK PATTERNS

DXCD

pack my

gizherst

nduowff

DESIGNS FOR UNIVERSITY OF CALIFORNIA OLD STYLE ITALIC
REDUCED FROM THE 2½-INCH WORK PATTERNS

to me too general in its scope, since the telephone directory lists hundreds of names for all sorts of things with some variation of the name Californian attached to them. I kept searching

ABCDEFGHIJKLMNOP
QRSTUVWXYZÆŒ

ABCDEFGHIJKLMNOPQRS
TUVWXYZÆŒ

abcdefghijklmnopqrstuvwx
yzffffiffllfiflæœctst
&1234567890"!?.-;:,$

ABCDEFGHIJKLMNOPQRSTUVWXYZ ÆŒ ABCDEGMRT
abcdefghijklmnopqrstuvwxyzffffiffllfiflæœctst"!?.-;:,&gvw

VARIOUS CHARACTERS FOR UNIVERSITY OF CALIFORNIA OLD STYLE

for some more euphonious designation that would be at once appropriate, simple, and not too long.

At dinner one evening, at Mr. Farquhar's, after my arrival in Berkeley to assist in the making of this book, I again brought up the matter of a name, as I felt that the child should be legitimatized, and I suggested a name so descriptive and simple that I am amazed it had not occurred to me long before— "University Old Style"—what could be better? Mr. Farquhar liked it, but insisted that it ought also to designate *what* university by adding "of California" after the word University, and thereby it lost the element of shortness. I countered by suggesting that "of C" within parentheses would retain a degree of shortness that I felt was desirable, but he intimated that there are other universities—Columbia, or Chicago, for example—with names which when abbreviated and beginning with the letter "C" would leave the paternity of this type in doubt. I therefore withdrew my objection, reserving in my own mind the hope that the type I have made for the University of California might prove so distinctive that the mere mention of "University Old Style" would be enough at once to identify it as the exclusive property of the first university press in America, if not in the world, to commission its own type face, and that its use herein would serve also to preserve to posterity the name of its designer.

VII : The Design of Types

IT IS still a matter of conjecture whether Johann Gutenberg was the first to conceive the principle of casting movable [i.e., separate] metal types which he could arrange in words and sentences so that he could impress their faces on paper. There is, however, hardly a doubt, judging at least from the evidence available, that he was the first to make practical use of the idea, and that it is due to his ingenious application of it that the profound art of typography was born.

Whether he cast his letters in molds of sand or in metal matrices, is a question not really material at this time; it is the far-reaching results of his inspiration that most concern us in this discussion. It seems quite probable that Gutenberg at first had little more in mind than a desire to find some expedient by which to supplement with explanatory text the illustrations cut on wood blocks—some method that would avoid the labor of engraving the text itself, some device that would produce more quickly the pages which until then had been written by hand, some device that would supply a new and swifter method of intellectual expression.

I like to think that his chance thought straying through an idle reverie, a dream most golden, "a dream come true," became the author and originator of a power unequaled by any other single force in the world's history. Whatever his primary purpose may have been, printing from movable types soon superseded both the printing of engraved texts and the handwork of the scribes. Printing itself became primate. Today, the design of types has come to occupy an important place in the art of typography, a place fully as important, I believe, as their arrangement on the printed page of a book.

Mr. Lawrence C. Wroth recently said that the "settlement of controversy on the grounds of high probability leaves the student of early printing a mind free for reflection upon certain mechanical aspects of the invention . . ." but I might wish that he had carried his remarks beyond a historical perspective & presented to us a picture of the far-reaching results of those "mechanical aspects" he refers to, instead of devoting his attention so completely to "the subject matter of the books that came into being through its operation."

Printing took over from the manuscript books little more than a tradition of marginal proportions and a basic form of letters which had been highly developed by the ninth-century scribes; types followed their forms in the main, unnecessary parts and mere accidents of handling were gradually eliminated, weights of stems and curves were harmonized, serifs were standardized; and these changed characters developed finally into forms in metal that now hardly betray their origin. For practically five hundred years, artists and craftsmen have worked to impart to type forms a new quality of interest and beauty and still to retain in them all the force of sound tradition.

Each new type face is heralded as an "original design." At once arises the query, What is an original type design? I should like at this point to outline here the conclusions I have formed after many years devoted to the study and practice of type designing. I feel that the ability to carry out personally every detail of drawing, pattern making, matrix engraving, the composition, too, of the completed types, the designing of more than one hundred type faces, and the writing of many articles

on the subject, qualifies me, or at least encourages me, to present those conclusions, asking only from all men pity, and of
the angels, power. Whether or not the reader agrees with my
conclusions, or whether or not he cares for my types, is immaterial; they are at any rate the results of long experience
and serious study.

What, then, is original type design? Is it possible for an artist
to design an original face of type? Probably not, in the strictest
sense of the words, since, after all, what we call an "original
type face" is undoubtedly little more than a subtle variation
of an orthodox or traditional letter form, a form to which we
attempt to impart a charm of character or a quality of personality—our efforts sometimes achieving a measure of unconscious originality.

The basic forms of letters are fixed; that is, they have become classic. When we speak of design, we commonly mean
invention, but since whatever already exists cannot be rein-
vented, we cannot reasonably expect any striking departures
in the design of individual letters. New or radically changed
forms of letters would force on readers a new literary currency
as a means of intellectual exchange. Nevertheless, we may give
to one face of type a quality of distinction, or of novelty in
mass, which differs from the quality presented by another face
of the same general character similarly employed, and it is
this difference in expression exhibited by the two faces that
I call design. I do not mean, however, that every individual
letter must present some actual and demonstrable difference
of outline and appearance, or even that it need exhibit a different set of proportional measurements when compared with
other existing forms of the same letters.

Nor do I intend to imply that we should make no attempt to strike out on new paths, since by the fusing of selected elements from two or more traditional forms we might possibly

"Types to they that be of the Craft are as things that be Alive, & he is an ill Worker that handleth them not gently and with Reverence. In them is the

TORY TEXT, 24-POINT

In the best books men talk to us, open to us their most precious thoughts, & pour their souls into ours. Thank God for books! They are the words of the

DEEPDENE TEXT, 24-POINT

The Life & Works of William Caxton, with an historical reminder of fifteenth century England by Benjamin P. Kurtz Note on Polycronicon by Oscar Lewis

VILLAGE TEXT, 24-POINT. COURTESY GRABHORN PRESS

achieve a new and pleasing effect different from that presented by either; by fusing harmoniously some modern letter with one of the past we may produce a distinctive and new expression,*

* The illustrations above show how by very little changes, made by adding to the lower case of one design the capitals from another letter of similar character, a new expression is created.

and this may also prove entirely original in effect and with no radical departure in form or loss of any of the essential qualities of good tradition. To make a demand for greater originality than I suggest here is likely to restrict natural growth. The real ends of type design are utility, fitness, and pleasing readability; design means progress in response to changing conditions of life, environment, needs, and aspirations.

We see, then—if my contentions are correct—that design is not so much a matter that concerns the shapes we give to individual characters which make up the new fount of type as it is a matter that concerns the printed appearance of the page as a whole.

Quite frequently the unthinking reader confuses mere mechanical technique with design. Type design involves craftsmanship of a high order; but good technique alone is not enough. A design devoid of emotion, rhythm, and expression, yet technically excellent, merely betrays the fact that it has been produced by one who has nothing of value to express. To produce a line by mere mechanical deftness is one thing; to draw a line of delicacy and refinement, subtle and expressive, instinct with life, vigor, and variety, is something else, and can be done only by one who possesses strongly a due regard and feeling for these qualities. In any types of distinction, the qualities of interest and personality, beauty and charm, are essential, and when the type exhibits them, fine technique, while desirable, is of secondary importance.

Printing, "the nurse and preserver of all the arts," at its beginnings neglected to record the facts of its birth or early progress, and many details are obscure which, if at that time they had been set down, would have left us with less uncertainty and conjecture regarding those facts: in the matter of type design the same reticence concerning intimate details and methods of work by the early designers is manifeſt.

Moxon, writing in 1683, in praise of Dutch types, said he liked them for their "commodious fatness"—a fair sample of constructive criticism of the past. There has been a marked neglect by writers on craft to write of the esthetic side of type design; they have contented themselves with mere criticism of details of drawing, rather than with close study or analysis of the qualities that make one type distinctive and another commonplace.

Believing that in years to come many readers will find in the processes of type design and the intimate work of the designers of today the same intereſt that we ourselves find in the work of the early craftsmen, I am constrained, while still occupied with the problems of type production, to set down here certain details which I find general readers and many students are ignorant of, though they may otherwise be well informed, and by so doing I may perhaps supply valuable, or at least accurate, historical matter about the methods of today for the student of tomorrow.

I have no illusions about my own work; I make no claims for its goodness—only assert that from the firſt it has been the simple, conscientious labor of one interested in the history and development of letter forms as expressed in metal types, and that each essay has been an attempt to better the one preceding it. It is a great satisfaction and a matter of pride that in my lifetime some of my type creations have enjoyed a degree of popularity and success never accorded some of the monumental type faces of the past during the life of their designers. Nevertheless, with a measure of chagrin I must note that my influence upon contemporary thought concerning types seems to have been comparatively slight. I hope, however, that the impulse of my example may inspire greater endeavor for finer types, despite the melancholy fact that type founders and type designers are producing today types which vie with the atrocities of the Victorians.

Fournier, someone has written, could theorize and write history from his workbench; as for me, every type produced from my worktable speaks for me, and likewise is an illustration of the qualities which at the time of its making I considered most admirable, and each marks, too, at the moment, the culmination of my artistic aims.

VIII : The Designer's Problem

A HUNDRED-ODD years ago, type design was generally imagined to be a matter that concerned the letter cutter only. John Johnson, author of *Typographia*, published in London in 1824, wrote that the printer need only "observe that its shape [speaking of a type face] be perfectly true, and that it lines or ranges with accuracy, and that by noting certain mathematical rules the letter cutter may produce characters of such harmony, grace and symmetry, as will please the eye in reading; and by having their fine strokes and swells blended together in due proportion, will excite admiration." He says further that if "the letter stands even and in line, which *is the chief good quality in letter*,* it makes the face thereof sometimes to pass, though otherwise ill-shaped." Evidently, type designing as a profession or an art was not regarded highly in 1824.

Today the type designer who essays a new type which he hopes will be useful, novel, legible, and beautiful sets himself no easy task. He must compete with the productions of artists over a period of five hundred years. If he wishes merely to revive or interpret an existing face of a bygone time, and is satisfied if he is able to impart to it something also of his own personality, the result may prove not unpleasing; nevertheless, if he stops there, no great progress in design, nor any great contribution to typography, has been made. If, instead, he attempts to weld certain characteristics of several existing types, thereby creating a face novel enough to pass muster, his work still has probably not achieved the highest plane. If his goal

* The italics are mine, not Johnson's. F. W. G.

[73]

is the successful production of an outstanding expression in letter-form, or the achieving of an effect in mass that will not be reminiscent of other types of similar character, the contribution of a letter which will not obtrude itself upon the reader's attention for its own sake at the expense of the thought to be conveyed, and which will, as far as possible, efface itself, his task is still more difficult; and yet, if he succeeds, he has really contributed something of value to design and typography.

Such a design will retain the imprint of the artist's intention and disclose clearly his personal touch even after it has passed through all the various technical processes involved in its making; it will reveal, too, that the inherent laws of good tradition have not been violated in his search for novelty. Its creation presents the most difficult task he is likely to encounter, and probably is completely solved only when art and craft are closely combined in one person. The infinitesimal peculiarities and subtleties which he will introduce into his drawings impart to a type characteristic qualities that almost defy analysis, yet the effect of their inclusion is quite clearly evident in the printed page.

Can such a result be achieved? Is it possible to design such a letter and yet not depart radically from the best letter traditions? I believe it can be done.

First, a letter is a symbol of unity that has come down to us with but little actual change in its essential form since the invention of typography. There remains, then, very little which may be changed, since we may not foist new or strange characters into an intellectual currency already fixed by long use, beyond giving the accepted norm a new quality of interest, or a quality of personality, and still retain the value of any letter as the particular symbol that must take its harmonious place with the other members of the alphabet of which it is a part, and, above all, present also a matter-of-fact legibility.

There was a time, in the golden age of type design, when a page decoration, a headpiece, a fleuron, or a new type might prove a key to typographical distinction because it was recognized as the work of a master and respected accordingly. This, however, is not to say that deference is to be given to old types of little merit merely because they are old. Many of them unfortunately have defects, even as do those of later date. Type may be good though it has not antiquity to recommend it.

Today the earlier master's art is revived, imitated, adapted, or reproduced [without apology] with cameralike fidelity, *prima facie* evidence of modern poverty of invention [or mental laziness]—a galling admission. The originals had matchless charm and were stamped with the personality of their makers; the reproductions almost invariably lack the spirit of idealism of their originators and cannot fail to betray here and there the fact that the faker can never do entire justice to the distinctive qualities that made the original designs great.

Our lower-case forms have a dual derivation, having descended primarily from the stone-cut letters of ancient Greece and Rome, and later—through the calligraphic development of them by the scribes' hands—having evolved into a variety of minuscules* which the ninth-century scribes had translated into pen forms from the most beautiful antique letters available. Our capital letters, however, derive for the most part and with fewer changes from the stone inscriptions of classical Rome. From the scripts thus formed the early type designers

* The source of our printers' lower-case types.

found their inspiration; their letters, of course, when translated into metal types, gradually lost some of their original
pen qualities, but only as far as the exigencies of metal engraving required.

The best type letters of the past follow closely and reproduce the characteristic calligraphic quality of the scribe's letters with respect to the thick and thin strokes which came
naturally through the scribe's handling of the pen, a quality
indispensable in the design of fine types. Since the first types
were made, for the most part only minor changes in form have
taken place, and those generally through attempts at perfection of details [i.e., in form of serifs, relation of stem and
hairline, degree of swells, etc.] rather than through an introduction of new features foreign to the ancient models.

In my own practice, speaking as a designer of types, I may
say that while my mind is consciously set on departures in
design, I am at all times aware that fundamentally my type
forms must be bounded strictly by tradition; I do not feel that
it is ever necessary to break deliberately with tradition to
secure a degree of freedom from rigidity or formalism. In a spirit
of humility [almost akin to fear] I attempt to stamp every new
fount of type I essay with my own individual handling of its
essential details. Critics unfamiliar with the classic forms of
the past too frequently confuse details of handling with under-
lying structure. They overestimate, in one design, some more
or less insignificant or flamboyant touch, and call that design
striking, whereas they rate another, less radical in drawing, as
mediocre; subtleties of handling may have produced in this
latter design a distinctly new expression in mass, but because
it is less obvious they wholly disregard it.

The type designer who is familiar with the development that has taken place in letter forms will soon discover what principles influenced the earlier artists and led them to produce the designs we now know and admire; in his own work the same reasons that influenced the early designer will probably occur to him also, and prevent artistic solecisms on his part. His attempts to solve the early artist's problems may, however, bring about some new or interesting treatment or expression in his own modern creation, and if so—he has advanced tradition!

In my more recent work as engraver of matrices and founder of the letters of my designs I have found that it is not necessary to repeat *ad infinitum* [*ad nauseam*] the mannerisms and peculiarities of the early types, nor even to make all types conform to an inflexible standard. It is more important to maintain a nice sense of harmony between letters of the fount with an eye to their legibility and beauty than to obtain conformity to any standard.

I feel that the proper standard of beauty in types resides, first of all, in their utility, but I believe also that there are secondary esthetic attributes which may be included in their design with no sacrifice of life and vigor and legibility. A certain rugged beauty is perceived without difficulty, and irregularities of handling which in isolated or individual characters might seem objectionable for lack of grace alone, might prove highly desirable in the composed line. Readability should of course be considered above every other quality, because failing this it fails utterly, regardless of every other excellence; but I believe that beauty of form should also receive almost equal consideration.

Early founders had no tools of precision such as we have; but the possession and use of highly accurate tools does not preclude the close observance of the principles followed by the early craftsman. Their use merely enables us to achieve more easily the freedom and vitality of the original design. We do not design by machinery, but we may reproduce our design with greater exactness by the proper use of the tools of precision. If, however, the machine is permitted to usurp the functions of the artist's handicraft, the death warrant is served upon a long-standing and worthy tradition.

If the designer who has reached a definite and recognized standing by reason of his study and achievements is to continue to produce distinctive work, he must maintain a complete indifference toward public opinion. Only by so doing is he likely to rise to heights of sublimity; the versatility and imagination displayed in his work must be his very own, not tempered by the suggestions of others; yet his work must be free from any trace of self-consciousness or the appearance of striving for an effect in his efforts toward an ideal.

ix : Details of Construction

IT IS A FACT well understood by every competent art-critic, that faultless precision of detail is the sure mark of mediocrity; anomaly, on the contrary, is the invariable characteristic of the highest order of genius."

Ambroise-Firmin Didot said of Fournier's punch cutting that it "was far from perfect in finish," and I have no doubt that the same criticism might be made of my own matrix engraving. I am more interested in the printed appearance of my designs as *types* than I am in the details of their manufacture, and I am not setting myself up as a matrix cutter or type founder in competition with workmen who have followed for years the various mechanical details of founding as a vocation. I care nothing for the criticism made of my work, since I cut matrices only to insure that my types will be artistic products completed in the spirit in which they are designed, instead of mere interpretations of my drawings by another hand. Mechanical precision, unless definitely necessary,* does not interest me beyond a certain point, and I maintain that simply by looking at a print from my type no one can say whether the types themselves were cast in matrices made by a type foundry or by a professional matrix cutter, or were cast in matrices cut by me. And if one cannot tell from the print itself whether the matrices have or have not that mirrorlike polish which founders so much admire, why be concerned about finish in the ma-

* This statement, of course, does not mean that mechanical precision in depth of drive, or line, or measurements of stems, and so on, is not necessary; in fact, the utmost precision here is of great importance. It is precision in drawing lines by straight-edge or bow pen that is meant in the present context.

trices? If the proof of my letter satisfies my eye, lack of "finish" is immaterial.

Why is it that one type is easy to read, whereas another that seems equally good in individual letters is hard to follow? Types are symbols which, properly combined, form words, and these in turn form sentences. They may be pleasantly readable, or merely readable, or even really illegible, and by "illegible" I mean that they do not permit the reader to grasp the thought of the writer with little or no conscious regard for the symbols themselves. But legibility involves something more than mere letter construction, since it depends on a number of items, and I shall not go into the general question here except so far as the letter forms contribute toward it, reserving my ideas on legibility for treatment elsewhere.

Letters must be of such a nature that when they are combined into lines of words the eye may run along the lines easily, quickly, and without obstruction, the reader being occupied only with the thought presented and, as far as possible, heedless of the letters themselves. If one is compelled to inspect the individual letters, his mind is not free to grasp the ideas conveyed by the type. If the designer can combine in his letters actual beauty of form [not mere superficial prettiness], distinction, delicacy, or vigor, and retain as well the quality of legibility, little more is needed. Ugly shapes obstruct the vision, not so much because they are not beautiful as because, though the reader is unaware of it, they divert his attention from the writer's thought and slow up the act of reading.

I have read somewhere that "types are not hatched out of type cases"; probably no one really ever thought they were hatched, but it is true that very few people do know exactly how they come into existence. The work of matrix engraving has never, as far as I am aware, been described in full detail, step by step, up to the point of casting type. Grant and Legros, in their excellent *Typographical Printing Surfaces*, touch on the various operations in connection with their descriptions of the type founder's engraving machines, but they do not go deeply into the use of such machines as tools to carry out to the ultimate the artistic craft of a type designer. They scarcely do more than touch on the preparation, for use in the engraving machines, of patterns that will preserve the freedom and feeling of the artist's conceptions in the finished matrix.

A number of scholars and artists—Lucas Pacioli, Albrecht Dürer, Palatino, Le Bé, and others—have written treatises on the shapes of letters for the use of calligraphers, but almost invariably their rules or principles are so burdened with artistically worthless and impossible geometrical calculations as to be of little real use to a designer of types.

For myself, I usually begin a new type with some definite thought of its final appearance, though it may be no more than the shape or position of the dot of the lower-case i, a peculiar movement or swell of a curve, or the shape or proportion of a single capital. From such humble beginnings I progress step by step, working back and forth from one letter to another as new subtleties arise, new ideas to incorporate, which may suggest themselves as the forms develop, until finally the whole alphabet seems in harmony—each letter the kin of every other and of all.

Disregarding any or all calculations, geometrical or otherwise, the designer has before him the problem of determining the respective heights of three principal items in his fount: first,

the height of his short letters or "middles," that is, those letters which have no ascending or descending parts, such as
lower-case *a, c, e, m, n, o, s, x,* etc.; second, the ascending
characters *b, d, f, h, i, k, l*; and third, the descending letters
g, p, q, y [lower-case *j* need only agree with *i* and *p*, and
lower-case *t* may be classed with the first or short letters].
The capitals [except J, Ꝗ] are classed with the ascending characters, but in my own work I rarely give them a height which is
the same as that of the lower-case ascenders, which amounts
almost to a fourth item of dimension. These heights are considered, of course, in relation to the size of the body on which
they are to be caſt, so that the extremities shall come within
and fill the type body. In my own practice, I make all these
heights on a drawing of each letter as though the type body
were exactly seven and one-half inches high.

Fournier writes in his *Manuel Typographique* that when he
has established these heights they are marked upon a gauge
of brass, sheet iron, or tin to serve as a standard, and I gather
from his description of the gauge that he made one for each
size of type he intended to cut, but that he uses the same proportions for those heights for each design. I pay no attention
to other designs in this regard, but make my heights for each
letter what I consider correct for that particular fount, and if,
by chance, the heights selected should approximate those of
some other earlier face, it is by chance only and not by intention, the design seemingly requiring those heights.

To obtain the heights referred to above, I usually draw two
lower-case letters, a *p* and an *h,* regardless sometimes of any
scale since it is easy to reproduce them in proper proportion
for my large working drawing when their proportions finally

satisfy me. I do not, as Fournier says one should, think of the letter as being divided into seven equal parts, of which three parts are to be allowed for the shorts, five for the ascending, and seven for the long letters and descending characters, but make each of those dimensions what I consider correct for that particular design.

If I were cutting punches by hand instead of cutting matrices in an engraving machine, a gauge that marked my original drawing in proportions and heights would no doubt be necessary.

While considering the heights of my *p* and *h*, I must also consider the weight of stem and hairline since these items have a slight bearing on the heights; next, the thickness and character of serifs; and then the height and weight of the capitals to go with the lower-case letters. Or I may start with a capital that pleases me because of some effect or quality in it, and once I have fixed upon its weight and height, I proceed to the establishing of weight and height of the lower-case in harmony with those details for the capital.

My drawing of the lower-case *p* permits me to strive for a movement in the round member—a movement that I attempt to retain throughout the face—to decide whether it shall be round or more or less oval in form, where the stress of color shall come, the ratio of stem to hairline, and a thousand and one matters that come and go in my thoughts as I draw. How shall the joining of the curve to stem at top and bottom be made, what thickness of serif, and what shape? If the face is to be "old style," the decision with respect to relations and stress is partly settled already, and if it is to be a "modern" face, while a different treatment is called for, the same points are also more or less settled in advance: the general characteristic of the old style is angularity; that of the modern face, roundness, precision, monotonous symmetry, with strong contrast between stem and hairline.

These drawings illustrate roughly the principal differences between the old style and modern faces, but do not show so distinctly the many and more subtle elements which may be incorporated in either form, and which will make one design

❡ Note the wedge-shaped serif at the top, the bracketed serif of descender, and the stress of curve of the bowl above center

❡ Note the thin unbracketed serifs, and the even distribution of curve above and below center of bowl

OLD STYLE   MODERN

distinguished, or by inept incorporation produce one more commonplace, although both may be intrinsically identical in their essentials.

It comes finally to this single rule, that the eye is the supreme judge of form; and the artist of taste who knows the history and traditions of lettering will unconsciously create these subtleties as he works. Taste may be developed by one who will take the trouble to acquire it by constant thoughtful study of those things which in the opinion of cultured judges have come to be considered as representing epochs of artistic history, of the best works of past generations that have developed by gradual modification into things equally good but belonging to and indicative of our own times. Taste changes, of course, but the things which have lived on and on all possess it, and even in their differences will disclose traits in common with their earliest manifestations.

Taste is the ladder by which we mount toward a greater perception of beauty by exchanging progressively something we recognize instinctively as not altogether good for something we recognize as less gross. Gradually our perceptions become more keen and we are able to distinguish between a good expression and an expression which is only vulgarly acceptable.

I show several drawings of some lower-case letters which more obviously exhibit in different designs the treatment of serifs and rounds and illustrate clearly and graphically what I have attempted previously to state. These are drawn to scale from original drawings for actual reproduction into types, proofs of which are given elsewhere.

We see that each has its own scale of heights of ascender and descender, of weight of stem and hairline, of thickness and character of serifs;* and whether old style or modern or text, the same thing is necessary, although probably influenced by different considerations in the various styles.

As each letter is drawn, I watch carefully to see that rhythm and harmony are preserved, since, as sometimes happens, what seems to be a clever conceit in treatment or happy movement just can't be made to fit in with its neighbors—and, painful though it be to do so, I take it out [hoping, of course, to use it in some future face]. When all the drawings are completed,

---

* I use my own designs which are ready at hand instead of attempting to reproduce with more or less difficulty letters from other well-known faces; to illustrate my personal practice in the technique of construction is really my purpose, not merely to exploit my own work as a designer.

I find it is well to lay them aside for a few days and then go over them again with a fresh eye; minor discrepancies over-looked in the glow of creation show up plainly now and are easily rectified. But I do not think a design should be gone over again and again, as this tends to tighten and stiffen it, to kill the spontaneity of handling that is so desirable. To do this par-

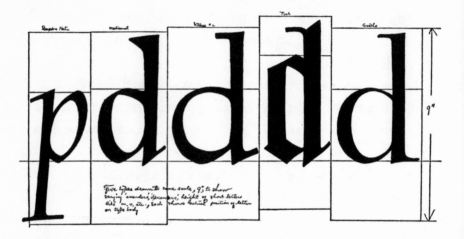

DEEPDENE ITALIC, MEDIEVAL, VILLAGE NO. 2, GOUDY TEXT, AND GOETHE, ALL DRAWN TO SAME SCALE. VERTICAL LINES SHOW FITTING OF EACH CHARACTER. TOP AND BOTTOM LINES REPRESENT THE TYPE BODY.

ticular design as well as I can at the moment and to do the next one better, if possible, has been my rule for years.

No rule can be given for determining the relative weights of stem, hairline, or serif, nor for the relative height of "mid-dles" and "ascenders"—they are interdependent, although these items may be indicated somewhat by the intended use of the face. It is difficult also to visualize a type design as type from a large drawing. In my own work I usually have in mind in general the character and weight I wish to produce, and I have so many drawings* in the same scale on hand that have actually been made into type that it is a simple matter to say roughly "a shade heavier in stem than some one of these, or with hairlines lighter, or serifs stronger, or the bowls rounder, or more oval, or the general effect more condensed or blacker

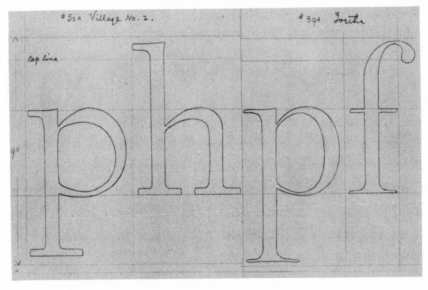

VILLAGE NO. 2 AND GOETHE, ILLUSTRATING DIFFERENCES IN
STEMS, SERIFS, DESCENDERS, AND BOWLS

or lighter," and with the dimensions of these drawings already exhibited in types made from them I begin with certain things already pretty well established. It is then that drawing begins. Capitals must not be unnecessarily self-assertive, or they will "spot" the page. A little difference in width of stem—a difference that may be measured only by a micrometer microscope in the type itself—will change the color of a printed page, and I am of the opinion that the wished-for weight is

---

* These words were written before the destruction by fire of my entire plant and equipment on January 26, 1939.

more often the result of accident than of deliberate intention. My study seems to prove the suggestion.

One of the most difficult points to determine is the "fitting" of each character, that is, the spaces between letters when they are combined into words. "Fitting" means placing the letter on the type body so that nearly equal areas of white space between letters will be apparent in any combination of let-

H I D J O V L T A

ters, regardless of their irregularities of form. The space be- tween two H's or I's or other straight stems manifestly should be equal; but what of the spaces between a straight and a round, like HO, or between two rounds, DO, or between a straight and an inclined stem as HV or HA, or between two inclined stems as XA or VA, or their combination with rounds, as AO, and such combinations as RA, LA, LO, LV, TA, WA, and others equally different? I draw each letter carefully within the space it requires, and a line drawn on each side of it repre- sents its "set" width in type as nearly as I can visualize it in a large drawing. [See UNIVERSITY OF CALIFORNIA OLD STYLE in chapter VI.]

Stanley Morison says of lower-case *a*, *e*, and *y* that they are always difficult letters to draw. I am willing to agree with him on *a*, but do not find any particular difficulty in drawing *e* or *y*. I suspect he means that unless the *e* has a bar more or less horizontal—not inclined, as I prefer it in old-style faces—it cannot be either good or correct.* Lower-case *y* is difficult to make so that it will not appear to "rain" tails through a page

---

* I refer specifically to the roman lower case, not the italic *e*.

if the tail of the letter is not just right in length and shape. If I were to plead trouble with any letter it would probably be the g, a mere "twiddle" of the pen at best, but a delightful twiddle nevertheless. Caps X, M, and W give me more trouble than other letters; caps Z, Q, and the character & I like to play with.

x : Making the Patterns

WHEN the original drawings have been made, capitals, lower case, points, and figures [and usually for a book type in sizes up to eighteen-point, small capitals also], and each character has been drawn as accurately as possible with regard to line, weight of stems, hairlines, and serifs, the next step is the making of a pattern that will retain the subtleties and disciplined freedom of the original drawings.

When I decided to become a type founder in fact instead of in name only, and actually to produce my own designs instead of having the work done by other hands, I tried a number of methods before I succeeded in making the simple and efficient pattern I use today. Since the pattern is exposed to considerable wear and tear, even though in my own work it is usually used but once, it must be of a rather rigid material, so that the tracing point which translates it into a reduced metal pattern will not indent or burr its outlines as it is guided against the pattern walls.

At first I tried various materials, a hard smooth fiber, of "bakelite" or similar material, in sheets; on these I would trace my drawings and cut out the letter with a small power jigsaw. This I found did not always give an entirely accurate facsimile of the drawing, since for a letter seven and one-half inches high I wished to limit any inaccuracies within one-hundredth of an inch, and my sawed-out pattern letters required more work with knife and file before they approximated the precision I sought. When a letter finally satisfied me, the sheet in which the letters had been cut was mounted on another sheet of the same material with paste or glue, which because of the extent of surface to be covered would not always hold securely, owing to the partial drying out of the glue on some parts while it was being applied on others. But even when the patterns seemed amply correct, a condition developed which precluded the use of fiber or "bakelite," as they proved unstable under varying atmospheric conditions; on a damp, humid day the height dimension might increase a thirty-second of an inch or more over the measurement of the same dimension on a dry day, depending on the condition when the tracing was made. So that method was out. I then tried cutting letters in metal, but that required work for which I was not equipped; the soldering of the cut letter plate to the base plates quickly and accurately was too difficult for me without special equipment for such work.

The method which proved efficient, quick, and much more precise than previous attempts was so simple that I wonder now why I did not try it sooner. I selected a sheet of 4-ply drawing paper or thin drawing board of good quality and about 0.020 inch thick; this I cut into pieces about 8 by 12 inches in size, and on each of these pieces I ruled five parallel lines [the long way of the sheets], with a 9H drawing pencil, making the upper and lower lines exactly 7½ inches apart; these lines represent the point size of the type body [as though it were a type that high]; the second line from the upper one gives the height of the capital letters, the third the top of the lower-case x, and the fourth the base line of the letters, also fixing the height of the lower-case x. Each piece of cardboard carries the same five parallel lines, and, to insure accuracy for all, I make a little gauge as long as the width of the pieces of draw-

ENGRAVING THE WORK PATTERN IN METAL FROM THE MASTER PATTERN

ing board, with the distances between the lines clearly marked, and at a definite point, say one-half inch from the top, with a needle point in a handle for convenience, I prick marks through the gauge, making five holes corresponding to the distances between the parallel lines, and use these pricked points as distance points for ruling the lines on the cardboard. By making the upper line at a fixed distance from the top edge of the cardboard and parallel with it, I can use an accurate try square, with a thin steel blade and a brass head, against the top edge of my pattern paper to insure that all of the upright fitting lines are always at right angles with the parallel lines.

My original drawings are made to a 7½-inch scale and are drawn on the five parallel lines which are duplicated on the pattern tracings, and over these lines I superimpose the original drawings. To make exact register I cut small holes in the drawing paper at intervals through the guide lines. Through these I can see the corresponding lines on the pattern, and make the lines of the drawings come precisely over the similar lines on the pattern sheet. Holding the drawing firmly, so that its position is maintained, with a piece of carbon paper between it and the pattern sheet I trace the form of each letter very carefully with a hard pencil, lifting the drawing by one end now and then to see whether every part of the letter has been traced. Then I correct any slips or omissions I may have made in tracing. Before separating the drawing and the pattern sheets, I mark the set width of the character on the tracing as shown on the original drawing, because these widths later will show on the reduced metal pattern and indicate the set of the type according to the point size to be cut.*

* The illustrations on p. 99 will show clearly what is meant. Refer also to drawings of lower-case letters in the preceding chapter, p. 86.

While tracing drawings, I may find that some slight amend-
ment is necessary or desirable here or there, and the alteration
is easy to make at this time. Then with a sharp thin-bladed
knife ground to a shape that will cut clean, without burr, I
cut out each letter on the traced lines by hand, remembering
always that it is the open space left that finally will be the
shape of the printed character. It is important that the cut be as
nearly perpendicular to the surface of the tracing as possible;
the reason will appear later. In cutting the "counter,"* I take
care not to encroach on the counter piece itself, since it must
be mounted later in its proper position to complete the sunken
letter that results from mounting the cut-out piece of drawing
board on another sheet of board, thus creating a large pattern,
the letter itself in intaglio, with guide lines and so on, later
to appear also on the reduced metal pattern, which will enable me to place it in correct position on the routing machine
for engraving. In order to achieve the greatest accuracy in cutting my cardboard pattern I do this work under an adjustable
magnifying glass which carries an electric light to illuminate
the traced cardboard I am cutting.

I commonly use a 7½-inch master pattern [cut by hand]
and engrave from it a metal pattern 2½ inches high, or one-
third the height of the master pattern. Two and one-half inches
is practically 180 points [actually 0.001 inch greater than 180
points, a dimension so small that when it is reduced again to
type size the difference is negligible].† To engrave this metal
pattern I usually employ three cutting tools, each cutting a

* The counter is the hollow within the outlines of such letters as A, B, D, O, P, Q,
R, a, b, d, e, g, o, p, etc.

† A point is 0.0138 inch; there are 72 points in an inch, but their sum actually
measures only 0.996 inch.

different width of line and ranging from about 0.08 inch for
the largest to 0.020 or 0.025 inch for the smallest. This last
tool is ground very exactly and the tracing point must be precisely three times the diameter of the cutting tool selected, since
that is the ratio of the 2½-inch pattern to the large 7½-inch
pattern. I check the metal pattern very carefully to make certain that the correct reduction is made. For example, on the
7½-inch drawing I measure with a steel rule [divided into
hundredths of an inch] the width of the cap stem of the H on
my master pattern. This dimension divided by three gives me
the correct width of stem on the metal pattern; if a discrep-
ancy is found, I know then that the finishing cutter is not in
correct relation to the tracer—it may be cutting a trifle too
much or too little, and I must amend it until the width is exact
before I proceed with the work. This accuracy attained, I proceed with the cutting of the other letters. First, I use the largest
cutter that will rough out all the large parts, such as the stems;
second, an intermediate cutter that will cut hairlines and other
small openings; and finally, a finishing cutter which will produce the finest openings, serifs, corners, and the like [usually
0.025 inch in diameter], and which by its accurate sizing will
make every part of the engraved character at the correct reduction and will retain every idiosyncrasy of my design as
drawn. This means also that no opening in the metal or working pattern will be less than 0.025 inch wide; and this in turn
does not permit the use of a tracing point, when engraving the
matrix from it, of greater diameter. To illustrate, to engrave
an 18-point type: this we see is just one-tenth of the working-
pattern size of 2½ inches; therefore, if we use as the largest
tracing point in the matrix machine one of 0.025-inch diameter,

our cutting tool must be in the same ratio, or 0.0025 inch. In practice, I make use of the slide rule to determine the size of cutters, reckoning the type sizes in thousandths of an inch rather than in points. By a simple equation—type size desired [say 14 points or 0.1932 inch] is to 2.50 inches [pattern size] as x is to diameter of tracing point [in this case probably 0.030 inch, the size I most frequently employ]—I find that I require a tool that will cut a line not more than 0.00231+ inch in width.

The pattern-engraving machine I use is a simple one, made for me in Munich. It is of the horizontal pantographic type, very accurate and capable of fine adjustment for depth of cut as well as size in relation to the master pattern I have described herein. The illustration shows its general character clearly. The master pattern is fastened on the upper table, the upper edge of the pattern against a straightedge so that each engraved letter will occupy the same relative position, and the tracing point, which is usually a rod of hardened steel about four inches long and approximately one-fourth inch in diameter, fitting snugly into the end of the long arm of the pantograph. Each end of the tracer rod is ground exactly to a certain number of thousandths of an inch in diameter; there are a number of these tracers, the diameter being, at its smallest, about 0.025 inch, and increasing by 0.005 up to 0.2 inch. On the lower table at the left a smooth tablet or plate of type metal about 3½ inches by 4½ inches by ⅛ inch is locked against a straightedge under a rapidly revolving cutter which has been ground to cut a line in a ratio of one to three with the diameter of the tracer selected, as mentioned earlier. These type-metal tablets I cast by hand in a stereotyping box. [Note pattern-engraving machine, p. 93.]

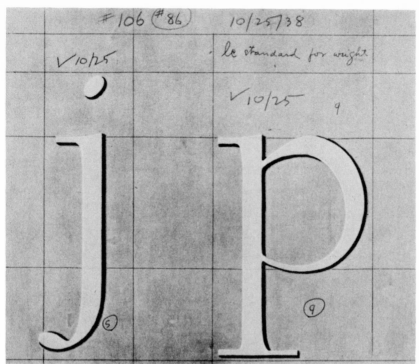

PAPER MASTER PATTERN FOR UNIVERSITY OF CALIFORNIA OLD STYLE [REDUCED]

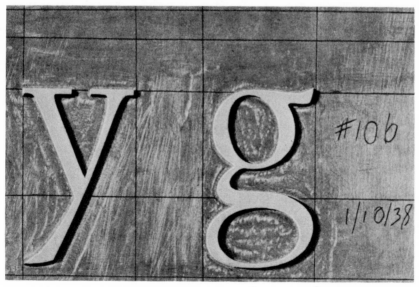

METAL WORKING PATTERN [EXACT SIZE]

Before beginning the actual engraving, I place in the long arm a tracer which has been ground to a fine point, and in place of the cutter I put a blank cutter which likewise is ground to a point. By moving the tracing point from one specific place on the master pattern to another place, such as each of the parallel lines on the master pattern [the fitting lines of each letter] and marking the type-metal pattern plate with the cutter point at the points indicated by the tracing point, I can scratch the corresponding lines of the master pattern onto the metal pattern in proper proportion. [Note work-pattern illustration.]

The next step after marking the metal plate is to relock it on the lower table, replace the tracer point with one of the proper diameter, and replace the cutter point by a cutting tool one-third the size of the tracer selected. The head carrying the cutting tool may be lowered or raised by micrometer adjustment; so by bringing the cutter down until it just barely touches the surface of the metal, and by adjusting a little device which allows the cutter to be lifted slightly from the metal, the micrometer depth control may be set so that a depth of 0.020 inch is indicated; by a reversal of the device mentioned, the cutter will then cut the 0.020 inch below the surface of the pattern metal. As the tracer is guided around the inside walls of the master pattern, the cutting tool is engraving an exact facsimile of the letter, one-third the size of the master pattern, in the type metal and in the exact position of the master letter with respect to the guide lines. I examine the metal pattern to see that the walls and the sunken surface of the letter are clean and smooth, and I stamp on the surface the work number of the design, the date when it was engraved, or any necessary instructions regarding some detail that might later be overlooked.

When all the work patterns are finished, I check them with
the drawings [to make sure none have been omitted] and put
them in a container [usually a cigar box], which I mark, for
identification, with the work number and the name I have
given to the design. I usually put with the patterns a memo-
randum giving the "settings" of the engraving machine, the
size of the tracer, and the width of the cutting tool, so that if
later a matrix has to be replaced, the work of making technical
calculations anew is avoided and accuracy is made easier.

XI : Matrix Engraving

FOURNIER says that "matrices are the fruit and product of the punches." In my own work, matrices are the fruit of my drawings, which I translate into intaglio metal patterns for use in the matrix-engraving machine. Fournier engraved steel punches by hand; I cut large master patterns by hand, engrave them mechanically in reduced size in metal, & from these metal patterns engrave the matrices for casting. In describing my method of engraving matrices I wish it clearly understood that I am describing a method which I devised for my own use. I realize fully that a type foundry or a composing-machine company operating on a large scale would find my method not entirely practicable, since it so largely depends on my own personal handling for its effectiveness, even though the principle involved in the actual execution is similar to that of the foundries—which are forced to employ, to carry out details of execution, operators who may be good enough mechanics, but who are not always competent to translate the designer's subtleties of line or design as exactly as he would like. My method differs more in the simplicity of its materials than in its actual operation, and I am not intending to imply that it is better than methods employed elsewhere; I maintain only that I have found it sufficiently accurate, direct, and expeditious for my own requirements.

Before taking up the actual process of engraving the matrix, I would like to discuss briefly my own feeling about the ethics of the matter. I feel that an artist is unjust both to himself and to his public when he is content to present merely good mechanical reproductions of his work—reproductions which may not convey the vitality and personality of his own handling of them—and it is to make sure that my matrices are carried out in the spirit in which the letters themselves were designed, and to retain in them those infinitesimal qualities of feeling which only the designer may give, that I engrave them personally. It has been said that to translate a book from one language into another is like pouring honey from one vessel to another—something must always be lost. Just so, the reproduction of a type designed by the artist but engraved by another hand is bound to lose something of the spirit of the original design.

The practice of any craft should be governed by common sense, and I mean here to refer to purely technical considerations rather than to speak of any esthetic qualities that are presented by the work in hand. You put your mind to it, you round your back to the burden of inevitable mistakes, and sooner or later you achieve the end desired. You do your best with tools which aid but which do not lessen the manhood of the user. I do not believe that it is the use of a machine or of machine tools that makes a thing bad—it is the evil use of them. Used as a tool, the machine minimizes labor which is necessary but which, in itself, is merely painful and monotonous. The most complicated mechanical device is justifiable if it aids good design or improves the quality of the product for which it is employed, but not if it helps to make machines of our souls.

In Part X of *The Colophon*, a book collectors' quarterly, the late Rudolf Koch, one of Germany's outstanding type designers, wrote: "The engraving machine is seeking to displace craftsmanship, and we must bring pressure to bear in opposition." Theoretically I am in agreement with his statement, but I feel that some qualifications are necessary in relation to certain facts which he does not bring into the picture. I cannot bring myself to regard handicraft as so circumscribed as he presents it. Why continue Nicholas Jenson's slow and painstaking methods of producing types—methods which were necessary in his day because he did not possess the instruments of precision available today? As well return to the tallow dip for our lighting or to the slow stagecoach for transportation. "Time marches on." Professor Koch was an outstanding figure in modern type design and type production. His craftsmanship in this and other forms of artistic endeavor was far beyond my simple efforts; but I do feel that he was in error in refusing to grant either art or craft to other methods in type production than the laborious cutting of a letter by hand.

Most book collectors are interested in every phase of the art and craft of bookmaking, but the majority of them are lamentably ignorant of the making of the types with which their pet possessions are printed. Many recent articles describe in detail the methods of producing the matrices in which the types are cast—carefully describing methods which, except upon occasion, have not been employed for years. Of course, the articles are correct enough so far as they apply to the types of the incunables and of books printed as late as the 1870's. But beginning [roughly] in the late 80's of the last century, other methods have displaced in this country the making of matrices sunk from punches engraved by hand; the older method persisted longer in England and on the Continent. I do not mean that punch cutting has been completely abandoned or entirely

superseded, but I do mean that punch cutting *by hand* is seldom employed nowadays for the production of hand-set types.
Punches, indeed, are utilized by the manufacturers of type-
composition machines, but they are engraved in some form of
pantographic router from a raised pattern of the desired design. These patterns, in the main more or less similar, differ
only in details of their making according to the user's pref-
erence. It is not this sort of punch cutting that I am criticizing;
I resent the continued implication that a type cannot be good
unless cast from a punch-driven matrix. Punch cutting by hand
versus matrix engraving by machine is a subject for dispute.
Certain critics maintain that a return to hand cutting is necessary if artistic merit in the type is to be achieved. To para-
phrase Hazlitt, "the only impeccable designers are those who
have never designed a type." I am willing to admit that if the
designer of the face also cuts the punch with his own hand,
he may secure a quality of handling difficult for the engraver
of a matrix to attain completely; please note that I say "quality"
instead of "excellence."

Rudolf Koch wrote also, "It can be said that unquestion-
ably the character of the old good types comes from the punch.
This is the plastic basis of type-cutting; since *it is impossible
even with the greatest care to make the form of the punch exact,** as
much more often, even with long experience, variations occur,
the result of counter-punching is always *a surprise** to the type-
cutter. Often the result can not be saved, and the punch must
be replaced by another; often, though, it can remain, even though
it falls short of expectations, if one has freedom enough to
make good use of the result. Such forced variations can come,

* Italics mine. F.W.G.

in the hands of an able punch-cutter, to a very beautiful result." Can it be that the beautiful types of the past are due to mere accidents of punch cutting? I am inclined to think that Professor Koch was speaking more particularly of his own achievements than of punch cutting in general.

When the punch cutter was also the designer of his type, proofs from the smoked face of his punch would indicate clearly whether he was approximating the wished-for form and color, and afford him opportunity to amend his work as he progressed until it did present both the form and the quality he sought. A print from the type cast in the matrices driven from his punches would show such a close relationship with his design that his handicraft would still be strongly felt in the typography of the printed page. But is it not granting too much artistry to a workman who may simply be a good artisan, to expect necessarily good design also from him? In modern type founding there are so many stages between the original design and the type made from it that the page becomes impersonal—the artist's feeling is gradually lost in the handling of various details of manufacture by the different operators entrusted with carrying out those details, and that is why I am not going deeply into the methods of others. I know my own work, its shortcomings and its excellences, and by confining myself to it I remain on safe ground.

But let us consider for the moment some of the steps leading to the making of a type from the artist's drawing. First, let us take up the original design, which, we will assume, has been made by one who has studied the development of letters and the progress of type design and who knows [or ought to know] something, too, of typography. He finds the design satisfactory; or at least it should be satisfactory to the designer. To produce a type from the design, one of four methods for translating the drawing into matrices may be used. First: A bar of steel is slowly and painstakingly wrought by hand at one end into a letter form which approximates his conception of one of the letters he plans to produce; this sculptured steel is the same size as the type which is to be made from it. While the workman is shaping his letter, he holds the metal now and then for a moment in the flame of a candle, and the deposit of soot on its face will enable him to obtain a proof of his work by impressing it on a sheet of smooth paper; when no further corrections are found desirable, the bar is hardened and then driven by blows of a hammer or forced in a hydraulic press into a bar of copper or bronze to form a matrix.* Second: A steel bar is engraved mechanically on a pantographic rout-ing machine by the use of a raised pattern of a letter which is, as nearly as possible, a reproduction of the original drawing; the resulting punch is hardened and, in the main by means similar to those employed with the hand-cut punch, driven to form a matrix. The pantographic router referred to is usually some form of the machine invented by the late Linn Boyd Ben-ton, or some variation of it, which utilizes a raised copper pattern around which a tracing point is carried, this in turn controlling the movements of a cutting tool which at the same time cuts an exact copy of the raised pattern and in any desired reduction. Third: A matrix is engraved direct [without the in-

* Of course a number of careful operations take place before our "drive" becomes a matrix, such as making its drive to a standard and uniform depth for each, the sur-face parallel and at right angles, the sunken letter correctly placed so that it will cast a letter properly in respect to position with its associates in a word; but I do not wish to go into too much technical detail not necessary here.

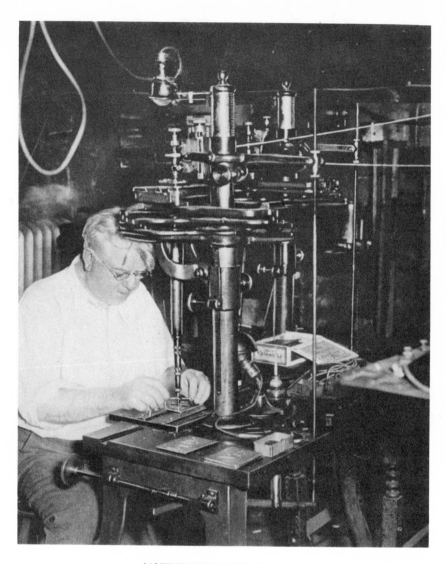

MATRIX-ENGRAVING MACHINE

tervention of any punch] in brass, bronze, nickel, or soft steel from an intaglio pattern of the letter, which reproduces the original drawing in any desired point size.*

For the engraved matrix a sunken pattern which is the converse of the pattern for punch cutting is necessary. This step has already been covered in the chapter on "Pattern Making." If the pattern has been made by the designer of the face, which is my own practice, it will of course be an exact copy of the original drawing in every detail and should preserve "the meritorious and human qualities of its original."

An article "On Designing a Type-Face" which I wrote for *The Dolphin*, No. 1, describes my method of cutting a matrix, and I shall quote from it freely since it covers the ground as completely as any changed or paraphrased wording could do.

The matrix-engraving machine which I found entirely satisfactory was not primarily made for such work, but with a few alterations which the manufacturer kindly made for me at my request it performed my work accurately; and—what was quite important—the machine, including the alterations, did not cost more than I could afford. The machine, similar in principle to others of like purpose, is a development of their common predecessor, the punch-cutting machine referred to elsewhere in this chapter. It contains an upright pantograph; at the lower end it carries a tracer which is ball shaped, and at the upper end a table on which a matrix blank is fastened. As the tracer moves around within the walls of the metal pattern, the matrix block also moves in a similar manner but in a reduced degree. Since the arm carrying the tracer moves in

---

* The fourth method is outside the scope of this chapter, since it consists merely in a mechanical reproduction by an electrolytic deposit of copper or nickel of a character already produced by one of the other three methods mentioned.

various directions to and from an absolute perpendicular, the ball-shaped tracer, being of constant diameter, maintains its center always at the same distance from the pattern wall, and relatively the center of the cutter is at the same distance proportionately. The upper end of the pantograph carries a table on which the matrix blank of brass, nickel, nickel silver, or occasionally steel, is fastened. The movement of the tracer at the lower end actuates the movement of the table above to follow exactly every movement of the tracer, reproducing the letter of the pattern to the size of type desired. The table rests on ball bearings and is sensitive to the slightest movement of the tracing point. Directly above the matrix blank is a machine head which carries a small cutting tool at the lower end of a spindle which revolves at a high speed.

This cutting tool bores its way into the matrix blank as the blank follows the movement of the tracer, and the depth to which it cuts is controlled by a micrometer graduated in half-thousandths of an inch. By setting the cutting tool so that its cutting point barely touches the surface of the matrix blank, the micrometer which controls a stop is opened up to the number of thousandths of an inch depth desired, and the tool is then free to come down, when lowered, to the exact depth it is set for, permitting the cutter to enter the matrix blank only just as far as the micrometer setting allows.

The cutter is one which I devised after long and tedious experimenting, standing at my bench, hour after hour, trying this and that before acquiring a workable cutter. Knowing practically nothing of metal-cutting tools, I began by attempting to copy a cutter shown in Grant and Legros's *Typographical Printing Surfaces*, but their description of it proved so much Greek to me. For example, what did this mean? "r the radius of the cylindrical face of the cutter $= b - c = 0.1445$ inch, d the height of the lathe center above the rocker center $= a - c = 0.1319$ inch, $m = \sqrt{(r^2 - d^2)} = 0.0590$ inch; $n = r \sin 11° 10' = 0.0280$ inch; hence $m - n = 0.0310$ inch and $m - n + q = (r \cos 11° 10' - d)$ $\cot 11° 10' = 0.0501$ inch; whence [illuminatingly] $q = 0.0191$ inch." For myself, I took their word for it and dismissed the whole mathematical nightmare from my mind, and continued my experimenting on a trial-and-error [mostly error] basis.

I drew a large circle, divided it into sixty equal parts [the reason for this number will appear later], and on it drew the plan of a cross section of the tool I had in mind, carefully noting various angles. I then ground a tool according to my plan in an accurate grinding apparatus, tried the cutter in the engraving machine, and watched its cutting action; I noted the "drag" or resistance of it, which could be felt as my hand guided the tracing point; I noted especially whether it was cutting smoothly and throwing clean-cut chips. At first it would break after a few minutes' use, and I would then just cuss and grind a new cutter, changing the angles of the cutting edges, all the while trying to figure out why it broke, until on one joyous day* I found I had succeeded in making a cutter, small enough and strong enough, that would cut clean; and furthermore, I could control the width of the line it would cut. This last item is the important one, since if the type desired is one-tenth the size of the working pattern, then the cutter must be exactly one-tenth the size of the tracer ball and the ball in turn must

---

* A day joyous enough in accomplishment, but tempered somewhat by the fact that I discovered too that the sight of my right eye was gone and I must perforce go on, handicapped by imperfect sight, in the performance of a craft in which perfect eyesight is none too good for the best work.

be small enough to enter every opening in the pattern, go into every sharp corner and every hairline. This meant that I had finally succeeded and could make a cutter that would, if necessary, cut a line one and one-half thousandths of an inch in width and strong enough to cut a depth of fifty-odd thousandths of an inch in hard brass. The end of the cutting point is, in fact, a very narrow chisel, the cutting width of which is in the same ratio to the diameter of the tracing ball as the type size is to the intaglio pattern letter to be reproduced.

Since the tracing ball and the cutting tool always bear the same ratio to each other which the work pattern bears to the point size of the type to be engraved, I contend that I can cut matrices for type from 8-point to 72-point from the same pattern and retain in each size the exact character of my original drawing, because each stem, hairline, serif, or counter is enlarged or reduced proportionately. For instance, this book is set in a 14-point type which I designed for the publisher of it. The notes are in a smaller size, the title page shows larger sizes, and all sizes have been produced from one set of raised work patterns which I engraved for the use of the Lanston Monotype Machine Company from my master patterns cut by hand from careful tracings I made from my original drawings. From these work patterns this company made the punches for driving the matrices.

To maintain the exact width of the cutting tool selected for the work requires constant examination of the cutting point under a high-power microscope equipped with a micrometer eyepiece calibrated in thousandths of an inch. I attempt to limit any inaccuracy in the matrix to not more than two ten-thousandths of an inch [about one-tenth the average diameter of a

EXAMINING MATRIX CUTTER UNDER MICROSCOPE

human hair] by stoning the cutting points in a special fixture that has a micrometer adjustment. My machines are then my tools, no less than the files and gravers in the hands of the ancient craftsmen; they enable me to translate my originals in a shorter time than would otherwise be possible, and I do not believe that anyone looking at any piece of printed matter can say positively whether the type from which it is printed was cast in a matrix engraved mechanically by me or cast in one driven from a hand-engraved punch.

The important point is to know where the handwork should end and the machine work begin, and especially to see that the facility of the machine does not tend to usurp or to displace any of the functions of creation and representation. The appearance of the work itself is of more importance than any quibble over the method of its translation into the vehicle of thought, since its legibility or beauty is determined by the eye and not by the means employed to produce the type.

I have spoken of a grinding machine and a stoning device which I use to secure precision in my cutting points. As this chapter is not intended to provide definite instructions on the manufacture of such tools, the illustrations will have to suffice. At one point in this chapter I said I drew a large circle which I divided into sixty equal divisions. These divisions correspond to sixty small holes at the back edge of the wheel which drives the spindle in the machine head carrying the cutting tool. Into one of these holes is placed a pin held in a bracket which permits it to slide back and forth, the end of the pin fitting into one of the holes snugly, and being so inserted as to hold the point firmly in place while the user grinds or stones the tool. The pin can be changed to different holes according to the angle wished.

My matrices are of three forms: first, the sort used in the
monotype caster; second, the form used in the Thompson type
caster; and third, the form employed in the automatic type
casters of the type foundries. When I began to look about for
the paraphernalia of a foundry I suggested to the late Mr. J.
Maury Dove, then President of the Lanston Monotype Machine
Company, of Philadelphia—an organization of which I was
Art Director [and still am at the time of this writing]—that

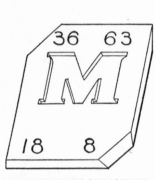

MONOTYPE DISPLAY MATRIX   FOUNDRY MATRIX

sometime I wanted to acquire a reconditioned monotype machine which could be adapted to my work. Mr. Dove at once
kindly gave instructions to place such a machine at my dis-
posal if I would say just what my requirements were. The
ordinary engraved matrix to be used for casting types for the
compositor's case, called a display matrix, if not driven from a
punch or electrolytically deposited from an existing type, would
not permit the close fitting I desired. I therefore decided that
special molds with trimming knives to remove the overhang
caused by the draft of the cutting tool used to engrave the
letter would be necessary. Also, the majority of the matrices
I already possessed, which, over a period of years, had been

MATRIX-CUTTER GRINDER

MATRIX-CUTTER HEAD IN POSITION FOR STONING CUTTER

cut for me by the late Robert Wiebking of Chicago, were all of the foundry form and of a different depth of drive from the monotype matrix, and casting from them constituted another problem.

After some months of designing, molds were made which would cast to proper depth, with knives to trim the types on four sides—top, bottom, and each side—and plow feet in each type as it emerged from the caster, producing a type in every way comparable to the best work of any foundry. These molds would enable me to cast from 10-point to 36-point. The two forms of matrices are shown here, reproduced from the volume by Grant and Legros mentioned previously.

The champfered corners permitted the correct registering of the matrix in the matrix holder of the monotype caster.

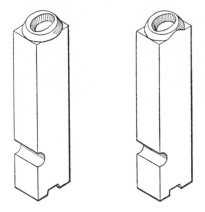

LEFT: A TYPE AS CAST SHOWING "OVERHANG."
RIGHT: THE SAME TYPE TRIMMED OR RUBBED

XII : Legibility of Type

PRELIMINARY ANALYSIS

ANCILLON, a seventeenth-century divine of eminence, wrote, "The less the eye is fatigued in reading a book, the more at liberty the mind is to judge of it. That, as the beauties and faults of it are more easily perceived when it is printed than in manuscript, so the same beauties and faults are more clearly seen when it is printed in a fair character, and upon good paper, than when it is printed on bad paper, or with a bad letter."

Volumes have been written, societies have been organized, a literature, even, has been developed to consider when, where, and by whom printing, or rather typography, was invented. Why does not the important problem of type legibility, also, receive definite consideration? Is it because we are too much bound by convention, and have a disinclination to tamper with the traditional forms of our letters; or are we deterred by a belief that the legibility we already have is as much as we can hope for; or are we inclined to let well enough alone, as it were, rather than to strive for easier readability?

To define legibility is to interpret an expression, an essential quality, a subtle attribute of type letters that makes some types more easily readable than others used in a similar manner or in similar matter; and to make such an interpretation is not necessarily to describe a definite characteristic of an individual letter form or to indicate some feature of it that may, by conscious effort, be omitted from or incorporated in its design.

While the designer ordinarily should not make letters as things in themselves, yet on occasion he may think of them for certain purposes as decorative abstractions to be looked at as parts of a whole—the warp and woof of a gorgeous tapestry that delights the eye by its richness. Here the greatest legibility is of secondary importance. Type has, in fact, two tendencies: one, to be a separate and independent achievement; the other, to serve an interpretative purpose. Both tendencies exist side by side, but one usually develops at the expense of the other.

Before I take up the problem of type legibility in detail, some preliminary analysis of the alphabet and its actual physical representation seems desirable, since many persons confuse "alphabet" and "letters." Although they cannot, indeed, be separated, to define one of these familiar things is not necessarily to define the other.

The alphabet is a system and series of symbols representing collectively the elements of written language. Letters are the individual characters that compose the alphabet, each being primarily a representative form. Yet each letter does have a secondary office—it represents a certain sound; but that sound is definitely separate and not affected by any peculiarity in a letter form. When a letter represents more than one sound its variations in this regard are indicated neither by its legibility nor by the lack of it.

The fundamental functions of a letter, we may say, are twofold, one absolute, the other relative. The first carries to the mind, through the eye, a recognition of what letter it is, that is, its name; the second, the part it plays in a word as spoken, that is, its sound; and both functions must be perceived as quickly as possible, that there may be no interruption in grasping the syllable [or word] of which it is a member. The part it plays in a word as spoken must be interpreted by the reader's intelligence, since the form the letter assumes gives no clue to the varying sounds it may represent in different words; for example, the word "the" is pronounced differently before a vowel and before a consonant, but no changes in the forms of the letters to represent these differences are necessary, as the rule for the different pronunciation is fully explained in the grammars and is applied subconsciously by the informed reader. Or again the sibilant *s* sometimes has the "unvoiced" or hissing sound as in "this," sometimes the "voiced" or buzzing sound of *z* as in "his," and sometimes is like "sh" or "zh" as in "sugar" or "pleasure." Its first function is simply to express the letter *s* and no other; its second can only be determined by its use, but as its pronunciation follows clear phonetic laws that we unconsciously observe, we do not, as a general rule, need new forms to indicate its value in its second office. The first function is the important one, and upon it the second somewhat depends. The form given a letter determines the degree in which it fulfills its first purpose, that is, its legibility, whereas the second is determined by its associates, by its position in a word, or by the varying relations of words with one another.

Letters are arbitrary symbols to which different people unconsciously give different values; letters themselves, however, are not interpretations of modified sounds, but parts of a whole. For the dictionary maker, the phonetician, the teacher of languages, new characters are needed that would be based on a scientific system of signs which would exactly define the spoken sounds—additions that probably would render our ordinary or usual reading alphabet entirely too cumbersome for general

use, and by their ſtrangeness compel slower reading. Many
letters, indeed, are phonetically useless and possibly might
be discarded, their places being given to new symbols that
would more clearly indicate their different sounds in different words. We should not overlook, however, the fact that
spelling affects the apparent legibility of a type very decidedly,
since we recognize words as units based on current universal
spelling. If that spelling is changed by dropping seemingly
useless letters, our text is made less legible. The letter *j* has
the same sound as soft *g*, but to spell "jug" "gug" would
attract unfavorable attention by its unusual appearance, and
its easy apprehension by the eye might be gained quickly only
by context. In words like "bight," "right," and the like, the *h*
is useful to distinguish the homophones "bite," "rite"; although *k* in the words "king" and "kind" has the sound of
hard *c*, it is more readily acceptable and more quickly grasped
than the old spelling "cyng." Before *n* the *k*, although phonetically useless, distinguishes several homophones such as
"knight," "night," "knave," and "nave."

A foreigner must find it difficult to understand how four
words spelled differently but pronounced exactly alike might
mean "true," "a ceremony," "a workman," and a verb express-
ing "literary composition," namely, "right," "rite," "wright,"
and "write," not to mention still another meaning, that of
direction—or to distinguish one side of the body [right] from
the other [left].

Possibly our present capital and lower-case letters might
be simplified so that both forms of the same letters would be
represented by similar shapes in both capitals and minuscules.
Since our minuscules came into use long after our capital let-

ters, which are strictly Roman forms, many of them differ so
widely in shape from the capitals that they could not have
been recognized by an ancient as bearing any relation to his
alphabet of majuscules. For example, note the varying shapes
of *Ff, Gg, Dd, Aa, Bb, Ee, Ll, Qq, Rr, Tt.*

A letter may not be considered apart from its kinsmen; it
is a mere abstract and arbitrary form far remote from the original picture or symbol out of which it grew, and has no particular significance until it is employed to form part of a word.
Theoretically we may, of course, consider a letter by itself as
representing a particular sign, but practically, only as a part
of the alphabet to which it belongs. We have, therefore, a definite duty to combat any attempt to interfere materially with
the accepted medium of intellectual exchange; we may of course
allow minor variations in the forms which are the daily tools
of written or printed intercourse, accepting changes if they
render the characters more legible. Variations are, therefore,
possible within very strict limits; no one has the right to impose some new symbol of his own devising in place of one
which is already accepted and agreed upon by the past generations and which has now become classic because fixed by
long use. I do not refer to the changes that come gradually as
a result of progress of the activities of life in all directions,
since they evolve naturally and are not brought about by mere
force or deliberate intention.

The references to phonetics in this chapter are included only
as they relate to the quality of legibility. The something that
affords quick and easy comprehension of groups of dissimilar
characters forming words and phrases which convey the author's
thoughts to the mind of the reader with no conscious intrusion

of the elements employed, that is, the letters, constitutes the particular quality which we call "legibility."

Conscious recognition of separate characters is compelled when an interest or beauty is interposed or substituted in the type forms themselves for its own sake, but it does not follow that we should neglect to employ properly related and proportioned units that are varied and harmonious and beautiful in combination. Type is rigid—it is the vehicle that carries the author's words to the mind of the reader—but it may, by its decorative handling, become itself the image by demanding attention and appreciation at the expense of the author's image presented by the type, thereby becoming indeed a "typographic impertinence."

The psychology of reading shows that words and phrases are recognized as entities and not by the spelling out of the separate letters composing them. Letters which individually seem to have all the quality of legibility do not always prove easily read in word combinations. No one will dispute the statement that type should be clean-cut and well defined [not over-refined, of course], & that the different letters must not remain isolated, but must flow naturally into words.

The early punch cutter made easy readability the great desideratum; if he could make his letters graceful also, he did so, but primarily his object was to aid the reader, not to display his own technical skill. How did he go about achieving easy legibility? What set of rules or principles did he follow? It is my conviction that the great types of the past exhibit beauty, character, and legibility mainly because their designers disregarded completely the matter of commercial necessity, because they endeavored to simplify and formalize the beautiful letters of the scribes with which they were familiar, and that by accident rather than by definite or conscious design on their part their types were made beautiful and legible. They had, of course, a clear idea of the shapes they wished their letters to take, the weight of stems, size, and so on, but I do not believe they had in mind any specific feature that could be incorporated which they imagined would bring legibility, or beauty, or interest. At this early stage of type making they had no precedents—they created them; they worked by feeling, and achieved results not in any sense an outcome of material-istic rules. But, whether by intention or otherwise, their types were simple in form; they showed thought in the contrasts of stems and hairlines and in the varying widths of different let-ters, and they were beautifully proportioned—qualities always found in an easily legible type; yet, paradoxically, no one of them, nor all these items by themselves alone, will produce legibility or beauty; there remains still the element of style.*

THE PROBLEM

FROM the far-off times of the Egyptian hieroglyphs to the nearly perfect characters of the Renaissance, letters were in the making. Today it remains only for the artist, by modifi-cation and new expression, to beautify the classic forms fixed for us by years of evolution and the stress of necessity."

In the choice of a type face for any specific purpose, the rea-sonable course, it would seem, would be to select, first, the most legible; but this is not enough, for types should be pleas-antly readable too, a quality depending somewhat on the abil-ity of the arranger of the letters, as well as partly inherent in

* The matter of style is more fully discussed in the chapter on "Fine Printing."

the letters themselves. Type arrangements may be simple and seemingly sensible enough in themselves, but if they are based on materialistic rules and not on artistic feeling they will lack still the quickening touch of life and variety. It is the function of the designer to make letters legible; but to make them be-coming, as well, requires that he possess also the taste and ability of the decorator. Legibility depends on three things: first, simplicity, that is, a form having no unnecessary parts [not the bastard simplicity of form which is mere crudity of outline]; second, contrast, as shown by marked differences in the weight of the lines composing the individual letters [stems and hairlines], and also as shown in the varying widths of different letters; and third, proportion, each part of a letter having its proper value and relation to the other parts and to other letters—these three things in connection with the aspects of purpose and use.

If legibility of types, however, is a quality inherent in the forms of the letters themselves, then the matter of spacing lines [leading], the spacing of words, the size of the characters, the length of the lines, and so on, are features which, collectively, add or detract somewhat, but are not the factors actually con-stituting legibility. In considering individual letters we know that the resemblance of some characters to others, the use of unnecessary marks or lines, the introduction of ornamental fea-tures not necessary to the form, all hinder the ready apprehen-sion of their significance; but aside from these points it is difficult to set down concretely just what is the particular thing that makes one type more legible than another. It is easier to say what particular feature may make a letter less legible; but, inversely, the omission or changing of that feature will not necessarily make it more legible, paradoxical as that may seem. If it were possible to decide just what feature would insure legibility, certainly no designer would neglect to include it in his drawing. Beauty & legibility are closely related, but beauty is an absolute quality whereas legibility is relative only and depends partly on the intelligence of the reader who is accustomed to read bad or illegible type. Less familiar but more legible types, introduced generally, would require an entire readjustment of the reader's perceptions to meet new conditions.

Types are made for use; but too often, in the attempt to meet only the requirements of utility, potential beauty is lost sight of, although utility in no way precludes the application of the fundamentals of contrast, proportion, and harmony, qualities that are absolutely inseparable from real beauty. The limitations of equipment and materials made the productions of the first printers beautiful because the resulting restraint and harmony compelled style. But we must not forget that it is the grandeur of many of these early types rather than their grace of form that accounts for the esteem in which the books showing them are held. The most famous books of the fifteenth century are invariably large books because the types are large. The *Decretals of Gregory*, printed by Torresani at Venice in 1498, presents the smallest sizes of any fifteenth-century types, the text being in bourgeois [9-point] and the notes in brevier [8-point]. Nonpareil [6-point] types were first cut about the middle of the sixteenth century. Gutenberg's Bible was printed in types that make four lines to the inch. The 1457 Psalter, a large quarto, has types of about two lines to the inch, and showing some even larger. They were "grand exhibits by grand men." Type forms inferior in gracefulness may still be harmonious with one another and combine insensibly into words, thus proving entirely acceptable to the reader because of their very power to form words which may be easily and quickly read. To retain this quality of legibility and to provide, as well, letters more graceful in form, is an aim worth considering.

Legibility requires proper contrast not only in the types themselves, but also in their arrangement upon the page. Readers resent [unconsciously] any wearisome inanity in type forms— a quality too often found. Some letter forms which are not intrinsically legible are made so by contrast with others of the same alphabet. Yet some types show so much of overemphasis in their contrasting features as to defeat the purpose intended, their designers having given, as it were, too much of a good thing.

In 1757, John Baskerville, an Englishman who was at first a writing master, then a japanner [a business from which he amassed a considerable fortune], still later a type founder and printer, attempted to improve the types and printing of his day. His types are distinct and show clearly the influence of his early profession of writing master by the thinness of his upstrokes and the thickness of the stems and the sharpness and fineness of the serifs. The contrasts are too pronounced; they properly belong to plate engraving rather than to metal types. They make a page appear restless and spotty. Even more noticeable in its contrasts is the type of Bodoni, Baskerville's most conspicuous follower, who printed at Parma.

Bodoni exaggerated the differences between his thick and thin strokes, and by the use of good ink, wide leading, and the elegance of his type, which stood out in beautifully marshaled lines against the white paper, gave his pages the brilliancy of a fine engraving. Good printing today demands the solidity of two facing pages forming an artistic unit, not pages presenting alternate stripes of black and white.

A reader accustomed to the ordinary book or newspaper types is likely to find them, or at least think he finds them, more legible than new or less familiar forms, but if the types to which he is accustomed were replaced for a time by types of greater legibility, a return to the first would at once make clear to him the meanness of a great portion of the types in general use. Assuming that the essential characteristics of the Roman letter at its best are fixed, what then is the first step toward legibility? We have already decided that no radical change in forms is possible or desirable; but very little change is all that is required. Letter making is a subtle craft and very slight variations make very considerable differences. It may not be necessary to attack each of the twenty-six members of the alphabet family to attain greater legibility for all.

At this point we meet the chief difficulty—how to reconcile widely separated ideas regarding the whole matter. Strange as it may seem, types easily read by one person are not always found easy to read by another of differing intelligence, nor is any argument advanced likely to convince against unthinking prejudice. For instance, the eye does not readily grasp a word if its meaning is unknown, regardless of the legibility of the types composing it. The unthinking reader might condemn the innocent type as illegible, not realizing that the fault lies in his own ignorance. The psychology of reading shows that words and phrases are recognized as entities and not as composites made by the spelling out of their elements, that is, the separate letters composing them. Letters which individually seem to have all the qualities of legibility are not always easily read in word combinations.

Reading is a process of thinking, a specialized mode of thinking through the eyes, but in the process the reader has not at any moment more than a limited amount of mental power available to apply to any one of the various details of reading. The type face which conserves and aids in quicker perception of the characters employed adds something to the amount of mental activity that can be allowed to the thought itself. To recognize the symbols that form the words read requires a part of the mental effort expended; to arrange and interpret the symbols requires another part; only the part then remaining is available for the comprehension of the thought presented. The friction of the vehicle itself deducts from its efficiency; therefore, the less friction the more legibility. A type is sometimes said to be less legible than another when as a matter of fact the writer's style demands a greater proportion of mental effort for grasping his thought than should be required, and leaves less than the necessary proportion for recognizing the symbols and interpreting them.

We think in particulars, not in generals; when an abstract thought is presented, the reader has to select from his store of images one or more by which to translate the author's words into the meaning of the thought; when the writer's style is obscure, a part of mental effort that by right belongs to apprehension of the type itself is diverted to comprehension of the message, and the type, though amply legible, suffers unduly; if the type, however, is really illegible, further delay is occasioned and a yet greater proportion of mental force must be expended, thus making reading still more difficult.

Type should be clean-cut and well defined [not, however, to the point of over-refinement]. Different letters should be so designed that they do not remain isolated, but flow naturally into words that will be easily and quickly apprehended.

That quality, possessed collectively, which insures quick and easy apprehension of groups of dissimilar characters forming words and phrases which are intended to convey to the mind of the reader the thought of the author with no conscious intrusion of the elements [the letters] composing the words and phrases, constitutes legibility, and is, therefore, not a quality inherent in individual characters. Conscious recognition of separate characters is compelled when an attempt is made to interpose or substitute a beauty or interest in the forms of the type themselves for their own sake; but it does not follow that the use of properly related and proportioned units that may be varied and harmonious will be illegible. Nor should the esthetic quality of a type as a whole be disregarded, as beauty is an element which in no way requires any sacrifice of legibility, since it is the inherent characteristic of simplicity, dignity, harmony, and strength, and is not the result of any predetermined effort to produce it. The units employed may be beautiful in combination although not necessarily beautiful when viewed as individual characters.

Type is rigid and implacable. It is the vehicle for transmitting the author's thought to the reader's mind, but it may, by its decorative handling, become itself the image, demanding attention and appreciation that belong to the author, and thus drawing attention from the author's image by subordinating the thought to the mode of its presentation. Clearness and beauty of the vehicle should not require a sacrifice of the thought to be conveyed. Yet to attempt to make each separate symbol beautiful cannot fail to draw to the types the attention that belongs to the message they present.

Beauty of the page as a whole is attained by the use of proper types and by taking advantage of a pause or break in the text for the insertion of some characteristic decoration, an initial, or headband, or possibly by the dignified and simple arrangement of the types themselves—never by making the types the main object of interest. Once in a while the decorative value of a line of lettering may take precedence of legibility [if not permitted to go too far], but letters should not be deformed for the sake of expediency, nor designed in unusual shapes without very exceptional artistic warrant.

Types may seem too prim or too stiff, but unless the lettering to take their place is of real decorative value and in complete harmony with the plan and matter where they are to be used, it is better to accept the primness of the types.

The use of "black-letter" [such as, for instance, Goudy Text], ordinarily considered as illegible, for a word or line enables

Aldus Tory Gaslon Morris

LOWER-CASE GOUDY TEXT WITH LOMBARDIC CAPITALS

the artist to present characters possessing color and compactness impossible in Roman letter; and this use is justifiable if the decorative quality desired is of greater importance than legibility. The "black-letter" without any increase in actual weight gives an increase in apparent weight, and thus we obtain vivid contrast with the Roman forms.

Most types lack spontaneity; all the irregularities natural to a craftsman intent on design and not on technique—those irregularities and deficiencies which are the inevitable signs of life and vitality and the sources of beauty—are usually lost in the effort to meet a demand for perfection. A craftsman must be credited with a certain amount of technical skill and must possess, of course, a thorough knowledge of the possibilities and limitations of the mechanical processes in which he is working; but when he has expressed in his design all that his mind conceives, then every stroke added by way of finish and refinement not really necessary to the adequate expression of the design itself is waste effort.

Most types are read by intuition; reading has become a habit, and certain symbols are accepted because characters more easily discerned or more quickly apprehended are not in general use. The present state of interest in fine typography makes it opportune to suggest a revision and recasting of some of these doubtful characters in the spirit in which they were originally created.

That the Carolingian minuscules, the survivals of the old classical alphabet, contain the essential root forms is generally admitted, and may well constitute a point of departure. Carolingian writing had for its models the best features of the classical hands of the sixth century; to them were added suggestions of contemporary French and Italian hands until, in the twelfth century, a degree of beauty and legibility was reached which has never been surpassed.

Experiments for determining the legibility of types have been made by institutions and individuals, usually, however, with separate letters and not with combinations of letters or of words. The effect produced by the main strokes of *n* and *t* in the combination "not" would certainly give a different result [read under the same conditions] if placed in the order "ton," and this statement in the main applies to almost any other varying combinations of the same letters.

It is a pity that the experiments have dealt only with existing forms [not always well chosen], and so far as the writer is aware, no suggestions for incorporating any results making for increased legibility by devising new forms based on the experiments have been made. Why haven't there been enlisted in these experiments the services of a designer who has given thought to the question of legibility of letters as well as to physical representation and their esthetic expression?

As early as 1509, semiscientific discussions regarding parts of letters were begun, first by Paciolus; and they were carried on by Dürer [1525], Tory [1529], Yciar [1548], Moxon [1676], down to the present, and all with few real results. The writings of Lucas de Burgo [Paciolus] exercised a great influence on the mathematical researches of Leonardo da Vinci when he was making his studies of letters and their design based on arbitrary proportions of the human form combined with geometric figures. Dürer was probably cognizant of Da Vinci's work and spent much time elaborating the same ideas, which Geoffroy Tory in 1526 still further developed. Yet none of the drawings or the writings of these masters contain any practical hints or suggestions for use in designing types.

Rules or substitutes for the artist's hand must necessarily be inadequate, although, when set down by such men as Dürer, Tory, Da Vinci, Serlio, and others, they probably do establish canons of proportion and construction which afford a sound basis upon which to present new expressions. Tory's simple assumption that there is a relation between the shapes of letters and the contours of the human body is no more erroneous, however, than the hypothesis that there is one ideally correct form for each letter of the alphabet; erroneous, because the shapes of letters have been in constant process of modification from their very beginnings. Indeed, the shapes of the letters in daily use are due entirely to a convention, so that in preferring one form rather than another our only consideration need be for the conventions now existing and the degree in which each satisfies our sense of beauty.

The extreme of scientific precision was attempted by M. Jaugeon, the chief of a commission of the Académie des Sciences of Paris in 1694, who recommended "the projection of every Roman capital on a framework of 2304 little squares, and on a congeries of squares and rhomboids and curves for lower-case and Italic letters." The late Theo. L. De Vinne said: "These rules and diagrams no doubt are *of some use to designers of letters,* but they have never been adopted by any punch cutter." [God be praised!] His was the natural inference of one who was not a designer and possibly not familiar with a designer's thought or methods.

Scientific tests of the legibility of individual letters show that certain forms are less easily identified than others, but prove no more conclusive than would the same sort of tests applied to parts of the human countenance—an eyelid or lobe of an ear, say, or some other minor part, which alone would be difficult to identify quickly, but the absence of which, or its exaggeration, in a portrait would at once indicate its importance to the likeness, just as a letter with its fellows forms a word easily read by context although it might not be so readily identified when ſtanding by itself.

Dr. Javal, in an article on type legibility in the *Revue Scientifique*, condemns the practice of sacrificing everything to regularity. He maintains that legibility is not dependent on leading nor on the height of letters, but on their breadth and spacing.

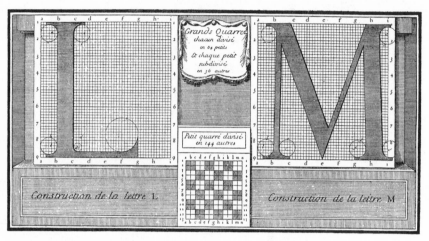

JAUGEON'S SCHEME FOR CONSTRUCTION OF ROMAN CAPITALS. PARIS, 1693

I am not prepared to accept all his assertions in full, as I find a certain "modern old style" type, more in use in England than here, to be more readable when leaded out than when set solid. I find difficulty in following the author in Pollard's *Fine Books*, although I am intensely interested in the subjeƈt. The type is unleaded and the white space between the lines is practically no greater than that occupied by the height of the lower-case letters, whereas the same type leaded in Warren's *The Charles Whittinghams, Printers* is quite easily read. I have never been able to complete my reading of Jennings' *Early Woodcut Initials*, set in the same type, for a like reason. I am inclined to think that Javal's idea regarding regularity presents the strongest claim to consideration.

In 1804 there was published an edition of *Rasselas* "printed with patent types in a manner never before attempted." These patent types, it appears, were invented by Philip Rusher, who substituted new characters for the descending letters *g, j, p, y,* to line with the lower-case *m,* a small-cap Q for the usual lower-case form, and all the ascending letters shorter than usual. In 1894, when the punches possessed by the Caslon Foundry [London] were being looked over, a package marked in indistinct characters "Rusher's Type" was found to contain the punches for the patent type of the *Rasselas* and consisted of the letters *b, d, f, h, k, l, fi, ff, g, j, p, y,* which were used with Caslon's English No. 1 on a pica body. Because so little care had been taken to give to his new forms the same weight of stems as in the face into which they were interpolated, the discrepancies tended not a little to defeat any idea of increased legibility which Rusher may have had, although they did permit very solid composition. At that time it was said of his type that "his capitals [with few exceptions] should be comprised within the compass of an oval. Each small letter is to be without tailpiece or descender, and the metal [both in capital and small letters] is to extend no lower than the body of the letter."

After a portion of the *Rasselas* was printed, Rusher for the remaining portions of the book improved the new letters used by making the stems more nearly of the weight of the other letters. For some reason he substituted a small-cap G in words beginning with that letter, retaining the new form when it occurred elsewhere. He evidently neglected to provide a lower-case *q* or was unable to cut one to suit his scheme, for in words requiring a *q* he used a small capital. I have recently acquired a copy of this work and I do not find Rusher's "attempt to correct a deformity" successful so far as greater legibility is concerned. Rusher's edition of the *Rasselas* is more interesting than beautiful; it will, nevertheless, always find a place among typographical curiosities.

> After this he lifted up his head, and seeing the moon rising, walked towards the palace. As he passed through the fields, and saw the animals around him,"Ye, said he, are happy, and need not envy me that walk thus among you, burthened with myself; nor do I, ye gentle ones, envy your felicity; for it is not the felicity of man. I have many distresses from which ye are free; I fear pain when I do not feel it: I sometimes shrink at evils recollected, and sometimes start at evils anticipated: surely the equity of providence has balanced peculiar sufferings with peculiar joys

RUSHER'S PATENT TYPES

In 1911 an investigation was undertaken at Clark University to ascertain "the relative legibility of different faces of printing types." The conclusions reached were [in part]:

1. Certain faces of type are much more legible than other faces; and certain letters of every face are much more legible than other letters of the same face.

2. These differences in legibility prove to be greater when letters are presented in isolation from one another than when they are presented in groups.

3. Legibility is a product of six factors: [1] the form of the letter; [2] the size of the letter; [3] the heaviness of the face of the letter [the thickness of the lines which constitute the letter]; [4] the width of the white margin which surrounds the letter; [5] the position of the letter in the letter group; [6] the shape and size of the adjacent letters. In our ex-

periments the first factor seemed to be less significant than any of the other five; that is, in the type faces which were employed in the present investigation the form of any given letter of the alphabet usually varied between such narrow limits as to constitute a relatively insignificant factor in the determination of its legibility.

4. The relatively heavy-faced types prove to be more legible than the light-faced types. . . .

5. The initial position in a group of letters is the most advantageous position for legibility; the final position comes next in order of advantage; and the intermediate or internal positions are least favorable for legibility.

6. The size and the form of the letters which stand adjacent to any given letter play an important role in determining its legibility; and the misreadings which occur in the case of grouped letters are of a wholly different sort from those which occur in the case of isolated letters. When letters of the same height or of similar form appear side by side, they become relatively illegible. But the juxtaposition of an ascender, a descender and a short letter tends to improve the legibility of each, as also does the juxtaposition of letters which are made up wholly or chiefly of straight lines and letters which are made up wholly or chiefly of curved lines.

7. [Refers to quality and texture of paper as not a significant factor.]

8. There is an urgent need for modification of certain letters of the alphabet. . . .

The following twenty-six widely different faces of type were studied:

American Typewriter	Clearface Italic
Bold Antique	Clearface Bold
Bulfinch	Clearface Bold Italic
Caslon Oldstyle No. 540	Cushing No. 2
Century Oldstyle	Cushing Oldstyle No. 2
Century Oldstyle, Bold	Cushing Monotone
Century Expanded	Della Robbia
Cheltenham Oldstyle	De Vinne No. 2
Cheltenham Bold	De Vinne No. 2, Italic
Cheltenham Bold, Condensed	Franklin Gothic
Cheltenham Italic	Jenson Oldstyle No. 2
Cheltenham Wide	News Gothic
Clearface	Ronaldson Oldstyle No. 551

Of these, omitting the boldface and italic types, as well as all capitals, the six best text types, ranging in average distance of recognition from 236.4 to 224.3, are News Gothic, Bulfinch, Clearface, Century Oldstyle, Century Expanded, and Cheltenham Wide. The six worst, ranging from 206.4 to 185.6, are Cheltenham Oldstyle, De Vinne No. 2, American Typewriter, Caslon Oldstyle, Cushing Monotone, and Cushing No. 2.

The tests were by distance, and types of 10-point size were used, but, with one or two exceptions, of the twenty-six different faces studied none were such as would be selected for printing fine books, not one presenting any esthetic quality or even approximating an ideal face.

RECEIVED NICELY
Brilliant statesman
gladly returns after
prolonged absence

A SAMPLE OF
NEWS GOTHIC

The conclusions reached are summed up in these words: "If legibility is to be our sole criterion of excellence of type face, News Gothic must be regarded as our nearest approximation to an ideal face, in so far as the present investigation is able to decide this question." [Ye gods! and has it come to this?]

The secret of "Caslon's Old Face" [known in the United States as "Caslon Old Style"] lies largely in its true justification—that is, every letter was cut as one of an alphabet, not as an individual; each member of the alphabet of which it is a part is in strict harmony and relation with every other. Since its production [about 1724] we have gradually drifted away from the canons of easy legibility. The reading public seems content merely to read, when it might read more easily; it tolerates bad type [occasionally good type badly set or printed] instead of demanding designs the chief characteristics of which would be simplicity, grace, greater legibility, and better arrangement of the types.

The Roman alphabet developed from the uncial on which it was based as a result of the scribe's endeavors to conserve time and space; uncial forms were displaced later by half-uncials in the lower case, the old uncials being retained for the capitals. Further changes took place, some logical and some simply the result of attempts to achieve greater rapidity in writing forms unrelated to each other in shape, proportion, or detail. They became a scribe's shorthand. When type came into use, many of the scribe's innovations which were mere habits of expediency might have been dispensed with, and more logical and more beautiful forms introduced or revived.

With this thought in mind, Charles Ricketts, an English artist, devised an alphabet which he called the "King's fount," in which he discarded four bastard forms of his existing "Vale" type in favor of four new ones based on the old half-uncials. His intention was in the right direction, but it seems to me that it was carried out ineptly, and this, coupled with Ricketts' own skepticism regarding the reception or appreciation of the innovation, may have contributed to its failure to meet the issue. In addition to four new forms of *a, e, g, r,* he substituted small-caps for *t* and *f* instead of redrawing or adapting older forms, and thus added to the rather confusing appearance when presented as a whole.

Robert Steele, in the *Revival of Printing,* says of the "King's fount" that "it is purely experimental, the first attempt of any importance to recognize that the printed letter is the work of an engraver, not of a scribe, and to free modern printing of some of the meaningless conventions of fifteenth century scribes in such letters as the *g.* Regarded from the point of view of design, this fount produces a very fine effect of regularity and beauty." It seems to me that this alone was something worth while. I feel that Ricketts struck the keynote and that the fail-ure of his fount was due merely to the fact that, through inept

> "Awak! awake! I bring, lufar, I bring
> The newis glad, that blisfull ben and sure
> Of thyconfort: nowlauch, andplay, andsyng,
> That art besid so glad an auenture;
> For In the heuyn decretit is the cure."
> And vnto me the flouris fair present:
> With wyngis spred, hir wayis furth sche
> went.   THE KING'S FOUNT BY CHARLES RICKETTS

handling, the idea itself was inadequately demonstrated. The Greek *e* as drawn by him is a disturbing form; the *a* has the advantage only of greater white inside; his *g* is not in har-

Haec honorum caelestium ad puellae mortalis cultı modica translatio uerae Veneris uehementer incendit aniı inpatiens indignationis capite quassanti fremens altius sic disserit, 'en rerum naturae prisca parens, en elementorum initialis, en orbis totius alma Venus, quae cum mortali partiario maiestatis honore tractor, et nomen meum cael ditum terrenis sordibus profanatur! nimirum communi n piamento uicariae uenerationis incertum sustinebo, et ima meam circumferet puella moritura. frustra me pastor ille

VALE TYPE BY CHARLES RICKETTS

mony with the other characters, as he did not base it on a good model; his R presents more of reason, but his use of the small caps T and F instead of older uncial forms seems indefensible. Alfred Pollard in his *Fine Books* says of Ricketts' face that his "good genius deserted him, for the mixture of majuscule and minuscule forms is most unpleasing."

A year or two ago I attempted to produce a type in which for my lower-case letters I drew on the half-uncials of the fourth, fifth, sixth, and seventh centuries, eighth-century uncials with which I combined majuscules based on the square capitals of the fourth century, and the rustic lettering of the fourth-century scribes together with my own conceits. This type I named "Friar," and if the type has any quality of interest it is in

The Roxburghe Club of San Francisco will again have the pleasure of having as its guest FREDERIC W. GOUDY ✿ who will speak on 'The Strangeness of Familiar Things,' at our monthly meeting to be held Monday evening, June 10, 1940, at the St. Julien Cafe, Battery Street, San Francisco ✿ Dinner two dollars. ✿ Guests are welcome.

FRIAR TYPE BY GOUDY. COURTESY JANE GRABHORN

spite of my audacity in bringing together in one design the various elements that compose it. [See illustration.]

In 1876 M. Motteroz, a well-known Parisian printer, decided that his eyes, strained by typographical practice and influenced by prejudice, looked at the matter of type legibility from a viewpoint which was not that of the reading public. By a series of experiments undertaken with readers entirely unconnected with printing he arrived at the conclusion that types are read with less fatigue if they are: [a] rounder, [b] more equal in thickness, [c] the upstrokes [ascenders] shorter, [d] each letter unlike any other, & [e] the long letters well proportioned to their own body. Following his investigation, he produced for his own use a new letter in which he attempted to combine the legibility of old-style characters with the greater color of the Didot type. But here his reforms stopped; he did not materially strengthen the hairlines or bracket the serifs. An English founder admitted that the legibility of the new types was "striking, as striking as their ugliness!" but that "the superior legibility is too dearly bought at the expense of elegance and beauty." Nevertheless, the Motteroz types were

CLAUDE MOTTEROZ was born in 1830, at Romanèche (Saône-et-Loire). As the descendant of an old family of printers he was taught printing, to which he added the practice of other crafts. In 1874 he established in Paris a large atelier for photographic reproductions by lithography, about which he has written two treatises deemed of high authority. In 1876 he devised this form of roman letter. He is the printer and publisher of many schoolbooks which have been adopted by the Municipal Council of Paris. As

THE MOTTEROZ FACE, FROM DE VINNE

chosen by the Municipal Council of Paris as the most readable letter for its school books and official publications—a conclusion that is not shared by me, since I do not find them essentially legible; I think the "striking" feature has been overestimated.

William Morris in a note [printed after his death] on his aims in founding the Kelmscott Press, says: "I began printing books with the hope of producing some which would have a definite claim to beauty, while at the same time they should be easy to read and should not dazzle the eye by eccentricity of form in the letters. . . . As to the fifteenth century books, I had noticed that they were always beautiful by force of the mere typography, even without the added ornament with which many of them are so lavishly supplied. And it was the essence of my undertaking to produce books which it would be *a pleasure to look upon**as pieces of printing and management of type." Morris was an ornamentalist, and it is significant of the man that beauty rather than legibility should have concerned him most; yet, in stating the specifications for the type he proposed

THE CRONYCLES OF SYR JOHN FROISSART, translated by John Bourchier, Lord Berners. Reprinted from Pynson's Edi-tion of 1523 and 1525. Edited by Halliday Spar-ling. With Armorial Borders and Ornaments designed by William Morris. In two volumes, folio. Chaucer type. Double columns. In black and red. 150 to be printed.

GOLDEN TYPE BY WILLIAM MORRIS

for himself, he named the fundamentals of a legible type: "let-ter pure in form; severe without needless excrescences; solid without thickening and thinning of the line, which is the es-sential fault of the ordinary modern type and which makes it difficult to read; and not compressed laterally as all later type has grown to be owing to commercial exigencies." He called his type "Golden" from the *Golden Legend* of William Caxton, which was intended to be the first book printed with it.

Morris studied Jenson's type, which he drew many times over before starting work on his own design, but he admits that the lower-case of his letter tends rather more to the Gothic than Jenson's—naturally enough, to one so essentially a me-dievalist. Comparison of the "Golden" type with the Roman

* Italics mine. F.W.G.

types of the Italian printers which he admired shows that it is heavier in face than theirs and generally lacks much of their suppleness and grace. His handling of certain details in some letters actually gives them an appearance of clumsiness. Bibliophiles welcomed it as a return to sturdy medievalism and the simplicity of the early printers, but printers and publishers said it was too black. It was legible and it was an innovation. With it and the Gothic face he later designed, Morris revived the art of beautiful bookmaking; certainly he brought to the revival a knowledge and skill comparable to that applied in the designing of the most beautiful books of the Venetian printers. Morris was, at least, the "apostle" of his time.

On the death of William Morris, C. R. Ashbee founded the Essex House Press and took over two of the presses and some of the workmen from the closed Kelmscott Press.[The writer of these lines plumes himself that one of the Kelmscott presses, the one on which the monumental Chaucer was printed, was once in his possession. It is now the property of M. B. Cary, Jr., in New York City.] Ashbee at first used a Caslon face, but in 1901 designed the "Endeavour" type for his own use, in which he incorporated the worst features of some early Venetian letters, features which both Morris and Ricketts had avoided; he introduced also some additional "experimental" forms. He seems to have had the idea that type is beautiful only as it defies easy reading, a vagary quite usual with those artists who lack knowledge of the principles of legibility and of letter design. Almost every letter exhibits some meaningless quirk or excrescence not necessary to its essential form. The general effect of a solid page as set by the careful compositor, in combination with harmonious ornament by the designer of the face, is dignified and not altogether unpleasing, yet in the opinion of the writer it is, withal, one of the most illegible types ever cut. True, the types are individual, but they preserve entirely too much of the scribe's whimsicalities—which may be pleasant enough in manuscript because constantly varied, but which become irritating when repeated in line after line of fixed types.

> ✎ Of the vellum series the following will probably appear in the course of the next two years, and with the work, it is hoped, of the artists whose names are appended, they having promised frontispieces. The issues will be uniform with the 'Adonais,' and the 'Eve of St. Agnes.'
>
> The series will probably not exceed 20 poems in all, and may contain Wordsworth's 'Ode on the Intimations of Immortality.' Cowper's 'John Gilpin,' Tennyson's 'Maud.' Hood's 'Miss Kilmansegg,' Coleridge's 'Ancient Mariner.' Work has also been promised by Messrs. J. D. Batten, Laurence Housman, Walter Crane, and W. Sargant.

ENDEAVOUR TYPE BY C.R.ASHBEE

The "Endeavour" type compels notice of its peculiarities at the expense of its subject matter—as the sample here given amply demonstrates, it seems to me.

On the authority of Falconer Madan, Major-General Gibbes Rigaud, in 1887, experimented to ascertain what combination of types and colors could be read most easily and with the least strain to the eyes of elderly persons with failing sight. He found that a type called "Franklin," a sans serif of almost uniform weight of stems and hairlines, printed in dull gold on a background of dark olive, gave the best results. Three copies of the Gospel According to St. John were so printed at the Oxford Press. One copy is lost, one only remains outside the Press, and it is now the rarest of all Oxford books produced since the fifteenth century. I have never seen a copy.

Aside from the similarity of certain features of some type letters, requiring subconscious thought to differentiate them and thus retarding quick apprehension, it is believed that the greatest obstacles to easy reading are nonconformity, over-refinement, high finish, too great regularity of curves and lines, and the elimination of the natural irregularities and deficiencies of handling which the designer disregards.

Though custom has fixed many of the forms now used, the customs of the ignorant should not be allowed to become the standards of the cultured.

SOME CONCLUSIONS

TASTE in the choice of types, as in other things, changes capriciously; the accepted types of the past century that have been put aside are again revived and displace modern types inferior to them. The very commonplaces of today once were innovations, and many types now looked upon as having only a historical or sentimental interest are, perhaps, intrinsically beautiful. It is to be regretted that the life of a good type should so often depend upon mere caprice.

Two features of typography are often confounded: first, the design of the types themselves, and second, the skill or lack of skill in their arrangement. Early types were almost servile copies of the best manuscripts obtainable and closely followed their malformations, yet seldom attained the grace of free penmanship, which was difficult if not impossible to carry into mechanically square types of metal. Often the punch cutter reproduced thoughtlessly the scribe's infelicities of form and handling, and the compositor made reading still more difficult by his abbreviations, misuse of capital letters, and inconsistent orthography.

Merit in types does not lie in mechanical precision. Letters are of irregular shapes in order that they may be more distinct. Old types are distinct, even when not faultless in form, as they were designed solely to help the reader, and not to show the skill of the punch cutter.

The designer of types should not forget that his work is to be reproduced by an engraving in metal, not written by the hand of a scribe, and although he may use the letter forms of the scribe as a model, he need not imitate them slavishly. Types should be systematized, and freed from the accidental irregularities of the manuscript hand—irregularities which when reproduced and duplicated in repeated type characters would prove irritating; but, on the other hand, types need not be so over-refined and so precise that the quality of freedom and life which gives character is eliminated.

Bernard Newdigate, in an article on "British Types for Printing Books," says that "the early printers took their inspiration from the best of the contemporary book-hands"; he then suggests a "school as the source whence the type designer and type founder shall learn to design and cut beautiful letter for his books. . . . Not indeed that type letter should be a mere reproduction of any written hand; rather must it bear nakedly and shamelessly all the qualities which the steel of the punch cutter and the metal from which it is cast impose upon it. It must be easy to read as well as fair to look upon, and besides carrying on the traditions of the past must respect the prejudices of the present.

"But only a calligrapher whose eye and hand have been trained to produce fine letter for the special needs of the printed book can have knowledge of the manifold subtleties of such letter and power to provide for them in the casting of types."

My friend and erstwhile pupil, W. A. Dwiggins, of Hingham, Massachusetts, who draws letters of distinction and character, says that "the artistic quality of a type-letter is determined by its degree of grace of line and proportion. The standards of grace and proportion are to be looked for in the natural motions of the pen. But the quality called 'art' is dependent, too, upon the artist's appreciation of the material in which he works—namely, metal. The draughtsman does not attempt to copy exactly the form of his pen-written model, but modifies the pen-form to a shape suitable to its final state—that of a metal punch."*

In the early days, letters were shapes written with a broad pen, or, like the Lombardic capitals, formed by strokes of a brush: the relation of the thick to thin strokes was not designed, but was a natural result—it made itself, and the work was kept alive by solving each difficulty or subtlety as each was met.

The designer of types cannot fail to find, as he works, new subtleties of form which he did not at first think of—to notice some movement of line or expression that pleases him, which he will use to modify or add to his first plan, and he will continue to do so up to the last stroke on the last letter of his design.

The final test that every well-formed letter must meet is that nothing in it shall seem to be an afterthought; each part,

* William still clings to the idea that types are the result of the all but obsolete hand-cut punch; or does he mean "metal type" instead of "punch"? Or maybe he refers to the composing-machine punch, quite a different thing.

at least, should appear to have been foreseen from the start, and its form to have developed naturally and not consciously.

In the designing of types as well as in other forms of design the designer must use the technical limitations of his craft to its advantage and not strive by mere trickery to master, seemingly, that which in the nature of things is not to be overcome; he should endeavor to express only so much as belongs to his particular work and nothing which can be rightly expressed only by other and different means.

Most types are constructed, not drawn. Ophthalmologists have made many experiments to ascertain at what distance from the eye any certain size of type should be held as determined by the angle with the retina it subtends, but the shape of a letter, which is more important than its size, receives less attention. It is regrettable that someone in this profession is not interested in the esthetics of types, too; the ophthalmologist is usually concerned only with the question of illegibility, whereas the artist is concerned with the problems both of beauty and of legibility. Working together, each moderating his demands and ideas to the other, with due consideration of the technical limitations of the craft, who can say what improvement might not be brought about? But until this occurs I am inclined to agree with William Morris that letters should be designed by an artist and not by an engineer.

XIII : Fine Printing

THE BOOKS which help you most are those which make you think the most. The hardest way of learning is by easy reading. But a great book that comes from a great thinker,—it is a ship of thought, deep freighted with truth, with Beauty, too."

Print, the medium by which the thoughts of men are made visible and through which all literature finds expression, may be merely good, or it may be fine in the sense that a work of art is fine.*

Bernard Shaw has said that "well printed books are just as scarce as well written ones; and every author should remember that the most costly books derive their value from the craft of the printer and not from the author's genius."

Shaw's statement, it seems to me, requires qualification, since the printer's art appeals merely to the eye while the communication it presents is addressed to the mind. The books he refers to as "most costly" include, most likely, some detail he neglects to mention—that of provenance, rarity, or happy circumstance, which a more valuable message might lack. Note also that he says "most costly," not "most valuable."

But great writings, being permanent, demand a permanent and beautiful typographical setting. Such a setting may be said to be fine and thought of as an art, as a means, even, to higher aims and higher ideals, when the words of the great writer are clothed so richly that the raiment becomes both

* I would here distinguish between "good" printing and "fine" printing. In fine printing, type, decoration, and proportion suited to the subject receive equally the most fastidious and scrupulous attention and care; particulars of the distinction will be brought out fully in the course of this chapter.

an interpretation of them and a tribute to their worth—when
the typography is itself so delightful that the reader may, for
the moment, forget its primary purpose as the preserver of the
legacies a great genius leaves to mankind, and dwell on it with
pleasure for its own sake.

Fine printing, therefore, is something much more than the
printing that may be entirely adequate and satisfactory for
commercial necessities, or even that printing on which the
craftsman has exercised a greater degree of care and thought
for technical requirements than the mere exigencies of com-
mercialism actually demand, or upon which more elaborate
details have been lavished. But in attempting to define fine
printing, to say what constitutes it, or to tell how to produce
it, I find it difficult to avoid the dogmatism into which writers
on esthetic subjects so easily fall.

Printing nowadays seldom even approximates the dignity
and breadth of style attained in the best fifteenth-century work,
because in that work the high standards set up always reflected
a definite aim toward beauty and order, standards that today
are in some danger of being lowered through a too ready ac-
ceptance of new and less lofty standards of art and beauty,
standards which are the outcome of adventitious aids and characterized by machine limitations in place of craftsman's ideals.
The work of those fifteenth-century artist printers is now the
noble heritage of every reader.

The instinct for beauty in books no longer requires defense;
yet so frequently does the emulation of machine-made work
please best that it seems worth while to consider seriously the
sort of printing that bears unmistakably the human stamp of
life and variety as opposed to the impersonal results which

are produced by mechanical means and which aim at other ideals of art and craft.

Machine work has its place. When the machine is used as a tool, as a means to an end, by a craftsman who wishes to secure the utmost control over every stage of his work and does not pass the fulfilling of technical requirements into the hands of mere artisans, the result may be comparable to that produced by hand, in spite of the limitations imposed by the machine.

Reading an ugly book is no more profitable to good taste than reading trash is profitable to the mind; mean and ugly typography is "a veritable larceny from future ages." And while fine printing necessarily includes a degree of beauty in itself, beauty for its own sake must not demand or divert the interest or attention that belongs to the thought conveyed by the typography. If print, however, presents a thought in monumental form suitable to its magnitude, its beauty makes visible man's admiration of that thought. Beauty in the things we use supplies, too, a demand of the mind and eye, and is especially a characteristic of fine printing. But beauty is an absolute quality and cannot be produced by rule of thumb; it is usually the expression of a free person's pleasure in creation. I shall attempt to define the term "beauty" as applied to printing more exactly a little later.

The ideal book is not a simple thing; it is a thing made up of many parts, each subordinate to the whole which collectively they constitute; a thing whereon the eye may rest with pleasure as we pursue the author's thought. The beauty of the ideal book is plastic; type itself is rigid and implacable; the pleasing adjustment between the various parts is difficult, yet essential.

Printing, in general, should consist of simple decorative arrangements of lines and masses that aid in communicating the message it presents, and the expenditure of thought and labor and care necessary to its production should be in direct ratio to the importance of the subject treated.

In the early days of printing the craftsman lavished his thought, and care, and skill on the presentation of a bit of worthy literature which we may cherish and enjoy today; his art was applied to things worth while. Today, the printer is asked to devote time, care, and money to producing works of ephemeral value, to publicity, or advertising, only a very small part of which, no matter how well it is done, escapes the waste-basket. Thus is wasted much of the time and thought and money that by rights should be applied to something more deserving of preservation.

Printing, apart from its primary function as the vehicle of man's thought, is essentially a decorative art, and the decorative quality must enter into any attempt at fine printing since it possesses an artistic charm that arises solely from the technical processes employed in its production.

In printing of the most unpretentious character the types may be well selected and their arrangement good; the capitals harmonious and suited to the type and text; the paper pleasant to the eye in tone and pliable to the hand, its surface kind to the types and not obtrusive with wire marks; the press-work adequate, the book itself altogether charming—and yet it may not be rated as an example of fine printing. To be fine instead of merely charming, the ideal book must include, too, a beauty of proportion, wherein the trained taste finds ever an appeal to delight; a beauty of form and rhythm in consonance, showing the hand of the artist in every detail; the well-proportioned leaf whereon the type has been handsomely placed, the lines well spaced, and the decorative elements of like origin with the types, cut with like tools and with similar strokes. The ideal book requires the use of the best materials in order that permanence may be assured, as such materials contribute to the esthetic quality of the whole by the feeling of pleasure they inspire apart from their use. In short, the book beautiful is a living and corporate entity in which each part is exquisite, conceived harmoniously, with true regard for the intrinsic requirements of the work seen as a whole.

In the ideal book, one part may be of supreme beauty, the others subordinate, each contributing in its own peculiar and characteristic way, yet permitting no one part to usurp the functions of another or of all of them—else, growing beautiful for itself alone beyond bounds, it ruins the whole. Nor should any detail of decoration pretend to be more important than the thing it decorates. Fine printing appeals to the eye, while the communication it presents is addressed to the mind; any detail, then, no matter how beautiful it may be, that interferes with the swift and clear apprehension or appreciation of that communication, or that draws undue attention to itself for its own sake, is misplaced and becomes thereby a typographical impertinence.

Let us attempt to set down some of the essentials of fine printing. First, it must have design. Printers, as a class, seem to think [probably not consciously] that it is possible to detach design from craft, and forget that design is itself an essential of all good workmanship. For years it was the fashion to look upon design as a mere matter of appearance, something added by way of ornamentation. Today it is seen that in its widest interpretation design is an inseparable quality of the work itself, and involves the selection of proper materials, and a realization of the work's purpose, as well as concern for its appearance. I therefore urge printers to consider seriously the elementary principles of design so that they may apply them in their work.

"Design," said Vasari, "is the well-head of all art; and in not having that, one has nothing." Design in typography does not mean capricious originality. It means reasonableness and natural growth, not an attempt to coerce the elements employed into some preconceived arrangement that may not be the natural outcome of the tools and materials used. It is mere affectation that arbitrarily places a line of type in one place when obviously it belongs elsewhere. Design, in the printed page, utilizes the printer's types and ornaments instead of the artist's abstract lines of pen or brush and is the inventive arrangement of lines and masses in such a relation to each other that they form a harmonious whole, to which each separate part contributes, but in such combination with every other part that the result is a unity of effort that satisfies the esthetic sense.

Second, fine printing must be simple in construction. It does not follow, however, that simplicity in any way implies poverty of invention, nor even the use of bare essentials only, or the tasteful use merely of ordinary materials. Simplicity does demand, however, the elimination of everything not necessary to the beauty of the result or the fulfillment of its purpose. Simplicity comes from straightforward thinking on the part of a craftsman to whom doing the right thing comes naturally because his work evolves naturally, not self-consciously. He does the obvious thing, or at least the result seems to be the obvious outcome of the materials with which he works; he makes utility the great desideratum, not artistic caprice, nor any illustration of his own skill.

Neither does simplicity necessarily preclude the possible use of some highly elaborate detail that contributes to the beauty of the arrangement as a whole—a decorative headband, an ornamented capital, or a line of lettering more decorative than prim types,—since these items usually are mere details of a scheme which in general may be of the utmost simplicity in conception. Where the eye may rest, decoration may appropriately be introduced and yet not necessarily detract from the simplicity of the arrangement. Print is really an apparatus which presents the symbols of language for the conveyance of thought, and just as with a mechanical apparatus, the simpler its parts are arranged the greater will be the effect produced.

Third, fine printing demands a type without mannerisms, one that is easily and pleasantly readable, masculine, its forms distinct and not made to display the skill of their designer, but instead to help the reader. Type must be easy to read, graceful, but not weak; decorative, but not ornate; beautiful in itself and in composition; austere and formal, with no stale or uninteresting regularity in its irregular parts; simple in design, but not with the bastard simplicity of form which is mere crudity of outline; elegant, that is, gracious in line and fluid in form; and above all it must possess unmistakably the quality we call "art"—that something which comes from the spirit the designer puts unconsciously into the body of his work.

It is one thing to ask for or to expect simplicity in the form of our types, but quite another thing to receive in exchange mere crudity of handling. Simple forms are desirable, but not if beauty is thereby sacrificed. Simplicity, to me, means the avoidance of affectation and needless complexity. Type forms may ſtill be elegant and at the same time be simple and beautiful in character.

Fourth, fine printing must have proportion, which includes such particulars as the size of the type face to be seleĉted, the shape and size of the page, the margins of paper that frame the type; proportion means, in general, dimensions and forms definitely related to one another. There can be no abstract or absolute rules laid down, since proportion is constantly changing in response to changing conditions and is the result of fitness.

And, fifth, printing may include all these items and yet not be ranked as "fine" in our consideration of fine printing as an art; it may still lack "style." Style is a subtle quality, inseparable from the tools and materials employed, and is the outcome of an intelligent use of a good tradition which is renewed and advanced into our own times, but which must not be permitted to over-ride the taste that personal expression requires, or be made the excuse for any failure to exercise that taste. Style is not attained by a preconceived attempt to add to types and type arrangements intended for one purpose a manner taken from those intended for another and quite different purpose. Neither is ſtyle simply a dress of thought or form, a robe to be put on or off at will; instead, it is the living expression controlling both the form and the vital structure of the means by which the idea is presented—a quality inseparable from the work of a craftsman wholly unconscious of style or of any definite aim toward beauty. It is that subtle attribute of printing which relates it to the time of the actual worker in the craft, as influenced by his environment and the stress of necessity.

Fine printing utilizes the beauty of the means fitted to the end of communicating a fine or beautiful thought; but at no time should the beauty of the thought be confused with the beauty of the vehicle that conveys it. When, however, the beauty of the thought is reflected or transferred to the typographical expression, the thought itself takes on new beauty thereby. The most beautiful printing is organic, a development of the construction; if it is not fundamentally beautiful by the force of the typography itself, it is only made tawdry by the mere addition of decoration. To make print beautiful is worth effort. But what constitutes beauty in printing? The beauty of an object, the agreeable emotion of pleasure it arouses, is perceived as one of its qualities and is one of the most notable of all the qualities which belong to simple objects. The beauty of the human figure is extraordinary, being a composition of numberless beauties united in one complex object. Similarly, in the printed page beauty is the sum of the various elements of proportion, refinement, taste, type arrangement and its decorative features, careful composition and adequate presswork, combined into one whole that delights the eye.

Printing is primarily intended, not to give pleasure by its beauty, but rather to convey the knowledge that books enfold. Beauty will, nevertheless, breathe on the dead types and bring them to life, and often enable us to see in the author's message a deeper sense than his mere words suggest. The term "beauty" in general belongs to objects of sight, as describing the quality of agreeableness, and depends entirely on an act of vision. It is ultimate. It lends its name also to express everything that is agreeable—a figure of speech, music, a thought. There is also, however, a form of beauty which arises from its use and aim, our nature seemingly relishing the appearance of anything answering adequately some good and useful purpose. Certain objects are beautiful in themselves because of their original purpose, or because their dignity enhances the pleasure we take in viewing them.

Beauty in the printed page may be considered as having two aspects: the intrinsic beauty, which is thought of for itself primarily; the other, the relative beauty, which is thought of when there is adequate fulfillment of the purpose intended in a pleasing manner. The first makes the beauty of the means the essential; the other makes it incidental; and both aspects of beauty may exist in the same work. The beauty of the typography should not be confused with the beauty of the matter it presents, but be in concord with it. The words of a song resemble in no way the music they are set to, as there is no resemblance between the thought and the sound; yet the emotions which each arouses resemble each other and bring concordance. There can be no physical resemblance between the typography and the writer's thought, yet the impression made by the typography may resemble in kind that made by the matter printed, so that the two impressions, being similar, mingle in one complex emotion of pleasure: when the impressions are directly opposed, the mind cannot receive them simultaneously, and the enforced unnatural union produces a disagreeable impression upon the reader.

A poem by Richard Le Gallienne in printer's lining gothic type, or a writing by St. Francis of Assisi set in a light-face italic, daintily printed in pink ink, would not render the writers' thoughts less correctly than more appropriate types and treatment, yet their obvious lack of concordance with the matter they present would be apparent to everyone. If one type, then, is more suitable than another for a given purpose, there must be some type most suitable for it, and the bookmaker interested in fine printing will not be satisfied with any but that right type.

But we must beware of the advice so often offered, that "the typography must express the character of the matter printed." It is a fine ideal; but there are dangers in the very principle. We must distinguish between concordance and similarity. A building should express the character of its purpose; but primarily that purpose is to house its inmates suitably and conveniently, yet not necessarily to express the character of the occupations its tenants follow.

Suppose, for instance, that the building is to house sweatshops or even something less noble; is the architect to tell the story in his work? Suppose the print is an announcement of a sale of antiques; must the printer employ old or battered types? Affectation is not art. The architect does indeed concern himself with the appearance of his work; just so should the printer concern himself with the appearance of his work: not that it is to be looked at for itself, but that it may give pleasure while fulfilling its primary purpose of communicating thought.

Concordance between the vehicle and the thought conveyed is not only desirable; it is also necessary. Notwithstanding the fact that mere words mean neither more nor less when presented in one type face than the same words when presented in an entirely different face, the types themselves may suggest to the perceptions symbols having direct resemblance to the things imagined, or some kinship to them. If the type selected corresponds in a way to the subject, there is such a feeling of fitness as makes that type more suitable than another, and there will be saved a part of the effort required to interpret the symbols employed, leaving more of attention to apply to comprehension of the ideas themselves. For matter dealing with poetic thought one should select a type less rugged than one better suited to a description of a steam hammer or an automobile; black-letter for a medieval subject; simple, dignified letter forms with no flamboyant features for dignified essays on abstract subjects.

Fine printing especially is expected to produce impressions of intrinsic beauty, but it must meet equally the requirements of relative beauty. The two forms of beauty never stand in opposition; intrinsic beauty comes from variety and contrast of the different parts harmoniously disposed in such a way that they contribute to the beauty of the whole; relative beauty presents a sense of congruity between the vehicle and the matter and gives an expression corresponding to the purpose, some expressions sumptuous and grand, others neat and modest, gay or splendid, a few monumental.

Intrinsic beauty and relative beauty are based on different principles and must not be confused. To illustrate: the proportions of a doorway are determined by the use to which it is put; a door for a dwelling is planned with respect to the height of the human beings who pass through it; and it may be relatively beautiful because of its pleasing relation to the building of which it is a useful detail, yet lack any quality of intrinsic beauty; the doorway to a palace or a great cathedral, in addition to its use, demands also all the grandeur and ornament consistent with the proportions determined by utility; by its harmonious relation to the building of which it is a useful part, its particular intrinsic beauty may help to render the whole building intrinsically beautiful and thus present an example of both forms of beauty.

Fine printing demands both forms of beauty to a degree not expected in a book given over to such matters as medicine, a work on differential calculus, a collection of political addresses, a machinery catalogue, any one of which may present qualities of relative beauty if printed thoughtfully. When the quality of grandeur, or of sweetness, or of power belonging to the message presented can be reflected by the type and arrangement, relative beauty is provided for, and when, besides, details are elaborated and made intrinsically beautiful without drawing to themselves the attention that belongs to the text, the whole may become intrinsically beautiful. Yet the most elaborate and pretentious piece of printing not appropriate to the purpose and character of its subject will fail to please the mind possessing genuine taste.

The printing of a mere advertisement or a simple narrative should no more be given the form or treatment of an epic poem or dignified essay than a farmhouse should be built to look like a city mansion, or a cottage be given the air and character of an ornate villa. Each has its own peculiar beauty, and to borrow an aspect from one for the use of the other is but to debase and falsify that other in character and expression. It is no more fitting to copy the arrangement, types, and "feel-

ing" of an old book or one produced under different environ-
ments and conditions of life and times, for present-day use,
than it is to copy an Italian villa and erect it on a congested
city street.

The great danger to be avoided is that of making the author's
words a mere framework or scaffolding whereon the printer
may exploit his own craft and thus allow his art to become
the end itself, instead of a means to an end. His duty is to
make comprehension easy for the author's communication by
the beauty of the vehicle employed, although not at the expense of the thought intended to be conveyed—the item of
supreme importance.

THIS EDITION OF TYPOLOGIA IS SET IN UNIVERSITY OF
CALIFORNIA OLD STYLE TYPES, DESIGNED BY FREDERIC
W. GOUDY FOR THE EXCLUSIVE USE OF THE UNIVERSITY
OF CALIFORNIA PRESS AND HERE USED FOR THE FIRST
TIME. THE BOOK HAS BEEN ARRANGED BY MR. GOUDY IN
COLLABORATION WITH SAMUEL T. FARQUHAR, MANAGER
OF THE PRESS, AND PRINTED AT THE PRESS IN AUGUST, 1940

This edition is a reprint of the 1940 edition,
and was photographed from a copy of the original printing.
It was printed by offset lithography at Publishers Press
and bound at Mountain States Bindery, Salt Lake City.
The cover of the paperback edition was designed by
Eric Jungerman, and is an adaptation of the case stamping
on the original printing.